FUNDAMENTALS

Also by Faith Winters

Abundance

Abundance Workbook

Connections

Connections Workbook

Fundamentals

Fundamentals Workbook

Keeping Calm

Keeping Calm Workbook

Restoration

Restoration Workbook

Trauma Healing Series - Book 1

FUNDAMENTALS

Escape the Lingering Effects
of Bullying, Abuse or Trauma

Faith Winters

www.FaithfulHabits.com

Trauma Healing Series - Book 1

FUNDAMENTALS: Escape the Lingering Effects of Bullying, Abuse or Trauma

Author: Faith Winters

Copyright © 2021 Faith Winters

First Printing: August 2021

Paperback ISBN: 978-1-7367367-4-6

Library of Congress Control Number:

Faithful Habits Press

www.faithfulhabits.com

Editor: Rochelle Dean

Minor portions of this book were originally published within other books by Faith Winters.

Contact the author at: faith@faithfulhabits.com
For information about discounts for bulk copies for groups contact: info@faithfulhabits.com

About the author

Faith Winters is a mental health professional with nearly two decades of experience. She is an expert who has taught thousands of people how to live calmer, more fulfilling lives. She is an author of books focused on helping people to heal and grow. Faith has mentored and trained many other mental health professionals.

Why I wrote this Trauma Healing Book Series

I grew up in an abusive home. The childhood wounds to our hearts and self-worth rarely heal on their own. They need some intentional help to heal. As a child, I learned ways to cope with the wounds. While those coping mechanisms allowed me to survive as a child, those same learned habits crippled my life as an adult and made each day harder than it needed to be. The wounds of the past were not healed, just buried. To heal I needed to learn the fundamental principles of how to live a healthy life that removes barriers to growth. Through a healing process, I learned how to value myself, how to have boundaries with others and how to find the freedom of wise decision-making. Now I live a calm, happy life with a calling to help others to escape the pains of the past.

God has comforted me, and I want to help others be comforted as they heal and grow. I want there to be less suffering in the world. My journey has uniquely qualified me to help others move toward a healthier life.

- **Experience in living for decades with struggles–** I grew up in traumatic circumstances and spent decades as an adult dealing with anxiety, panic attacks, and PTSD (Post Traumatic Stress Disorder). In the midst of those painful years, I learned valuable lessons in surviving struggles and the need for healing.

- **Healing process–** I went through psychoeducational classes, extensive reading, and professional mental health therapy. As my anxiety ended, and the panic attacks ceased, and the PTSD was finally gone, I wanted to help others to escape the traumas of the past and to heal and grow.

- **Education–** I then decided to attend university to get a master's degree in counseling so I would have the professional therapeutic skills to help others heal from trauma in effective ways.

- **Experience in teaching these key skills to others–** For nearly two decades I have worked as a professional counselor and have taught thousands of people how to deal with struggles, heal from trauma and live calmer, healthier, happier lives even in the midst of struggles.

As you learn more about your rights as a human, your mind may experience a shift from being a victim of trauma toward the possibility of a happy and healthy life. All of the principles in this book will help to build strength within you as you grow and heal. It will take some effort on your part to live out your rights and responsibilities, but the principles to move forward are here in your hands. If you apply these principles, it may literally change the course of your life and have a positive effect on people around you.

In these pages, I share the richness of our original design and how to remove the crippling effects of past traumas so you can heal. I provide tried-and-true methods for how you can make changes to let yourself heal from the wounds of your past and the fundamental principles of our original design of how we can heal and grow. If you address the emotional, physical, and intellectual principles presented in this book, you can have a healthier life. By learning and enacting the principles of a healthy lifestyle, you can live your very best life, unhindered by the debilitating effects of past traumas. If you learn and apply these principles, it can literally change the course of your life and have a positive effect on people around you. you will discover a revolution inside, a return to something even more powerful than happiness. That is the presence of peace.

Faith Winters has a clear grasp on the primary psychological challenges people face, and a ton of practical experience in methods that work with those who are most challenged by a history of trauma. She has phenomenal results and has helped more people than I can count. Her writing is understandable and usable. This is a "must-read" book!

William Russell,

Director Emeritus, Union Gospel Mission Portland

CONTENTS

PART THREE : FREEDOM FUNDAMENTALS

WHAT THIS BOOK IS ABOUT

Life is hard. The lingering effects of past bullying, abuse, trauma, trouble, or chaos can negatively affect today's relationships, today's ability to make good decisions, and today's ability to have joy. We may think we have put the past behind us, and yet the past seems to have trouble staying in the past. Often the feelings about the emotional wounds of the past drift into the present, making problems for today. It can give us feelings of stress, anxiety worry, anger, and feeling like bad things will happen.

Discover the difference between a life hampered by the lingering effects of bullying, abuse, trauma, trouble, or chaos, and a healthy life. Understand your basic rights as a human and what that means in a healthy life. Explore how to have more joy and peace within yourself, better relationships with others, and more happiness and contentment no matter what is going on around you.

Many people have experienced trauma and problems in their life that created pain and chaos and left lingering emotional wounds. The negative patterns of emotions and behavior that follow can last for decades since these wounds are rarely healed by time alone. Changing to a healthy pattern of behavior and giving those wounds a good chance to heal is hard if you are not even sure what a healthy life looks like. I have been there and healed from a traumatized, chaotic past into abundant, healthy life. I know healing is possible.

Fundamentals was written to give people insight into healthy ways of functioning and be more able to recognize the hindering patterns that develop in a life touched by abuse, and trauma. As the first book in the Trauma Healing Series, *Fundamentals* will give an overview of the primary principles on which a healthy life is based, the foundational groundwork of central importance. We will look at the rights each person has for themselves, in relation with others and with the world; and how these rights contribute to discovering a healthy fulfilling life. The next three books in the series, *Restoration, Connections,* and *Abundance,* will go deeply into the skill-building process for healing old wounds and moving into a pattern of healthy living.

YOUR RIGHTS AS A HUMAN BEING

In this section, I have organized our rights into the broad categories of individual rights, relationship rights, and freedom rights. In the three parts of this book, I discuss each of these rights in detail and help you build a foundation for healing from your trauma. Understanding each of these rights and living from a place that respects these rights in yourself and in others is an important key that unlocks healing from trauma and freedom from lingering effects of past bullying, abuse, trauma, trouble, or chaos.

Individual rights include how we interact with ourselves, the boundaries we set up and understanding what is our own and what is not ours. Individual rights include the basic ways we can expect to be treated and the basic ways we treat others, with dignity and respect.

- You have the right to be you and to love and be loved.

- You have the right to make mistakes, to be human – not perfect.
- You have the right to say NO.
- You have the right to choose your own values and beliefs.
- You have the right to your own feelings and opinions and to express them.
- You have the right to change your mind and your life.

Relational rights are the rights that we have as we relate to other people: family, friends, bosses, children, parents, neighbors, a significant other, and all the different people that we interact with in life. Relational rights provide healthy ways to interact with people.

- You have the right to be safe, to be treated with dignity and respect.
- You have the right to healthy friendships.
- You have the right to choose when and how your body is touched.
- You have the right to treat yourself as well as you treat others.
- You have the right not to be responsible for other adults' choices, feelings, and behavior.
- You have the right to feel angry and leave if you are treated abusively.

Freedom rights are the freedoms that we have individually and collectively to make our own choices of what we want to do and how we want to move forward in our life. These are the responsibilities and choices we have as adults.

- You have the right to your own privacy, personal space, and time.
- You have the right to make your own decisions about your life.
- You have the right to ask questions about anything that affects your life.
- You have the right to request what you want.
- You have the right to earn and control your own resources.
- You have the right to not be liked by everyone.

When we consider our rights as a human, some questions come up:

- How do we know we have these rights?
- Where do they come from?
- What does the word rights even mean?

Dictionaries define rights as the basic rules about what people are allowed or owed, being in accordance with what is just, good, or proper. Human Rights are the basic rights and freedoms that belong to every person in the world, from birth until death.

Another authority about rights is the Declaration of Independence of the United States of America. That document tells us these rights were highlighted as the rights the people when our nation was formed.

We hold these truths to be self-evident, that all men are created equal, that they are endowed by their Creator with certain unalienable Rights, that among these are Life, Liberty, and the pursuit of Happiness.

Further rights are discussed in the other founding documents of the USA, the Constitution, and the Bill of Rights.

Yet another place where rights are defined is in the document of the United Nations "The Universal Declaration of Human Rights."

Whereas recognition of the inherent dignity and of the equal and inalienable rights of all members of the human family is the foundation of freedom, justice, and peace in the world,

This author sees all these basic rights as principles that come out of the scriptures. These are the rights God describes and models for us throughout the Bible.

What we understand from all these authoritative writings is that:

As humans we have fundamental rights.

Limitations to our rights

Since ALL humans have fundamental rights, our rights and freedoms may end where another person's rights begin. Also, there may be times in life where, through our own choices or the choices of others, we may not have full access to all of these rights for a period of time.

Examples:

- When someone chooses to go into a treatment program or a recovery community.

- When someone chooses to live in a situation with others where these rights are not respected or regarded.
- Through no choice of our own, we are in a situation where these rights are not available to us.

That does not mean our rights do not exist, it means that for a while they are not fully available to us.

One of the examples is when someone chooses to go to a recovery community to get help because they are trying to recover from addiction, homelessness, trauma, etc. They have found a community that is willing to help them, perhaps without cost. But it is not a free hotel. The community is willing to help, providing a place to sleep, food to eat, and the other components of life; but there is still an exchange. So, when someone chooses to come into the community, they are also choosing to follow the program of those who run the community. So, for a period of time, they are choosing to limit some of their own freedoms and rights so that they can receive the benefits that the community offers. For example, in a recovery community, your choice of what to eat when may be limited to what the community offers. Your use of your time may be shaped by the schedule that the community dictates.

Learn about your rights

It is never too late. Anyone can learn about their fundamental rights as a human and begin to change their lives to live to respect those rights for themselves and to respect those rights for all those around them. It starts with learning about the fundamental rights of an individual.

Fundamentals:

The central or primary

rules or principles

on which something is based.

PART ONE

INDIVIDUAL FUNDAMENTALS

Individual rights include how we interact with ourselves, the boundaries we set up, and understanding what is our own and what is not ours. Individual rights include the basic ways we can expect to be treated and the basic ways we treat others, with dignity and respect.

- You have the right to be you and to love and be loved.
- You have the right to make mistakes, to be human – not perfect.
- You have the right to say NO.
- You have the right to choose your own values and beliefs.
- You have the right to your own feelings and opinions and to express them.
- You have the right to change your mind and your life.

This part of the book will expand on each of the individual rights above, exploring how we live out those rights, to help you to understand your individual rights as a human being. Also providing a road map of how you can respect these rights for yourself and respect these rights for others.

CHAPTER ONE

You have the right to be you
and to love and be loved

Each one of us is unique and different. Those differences are what make life rich and interesting. To live faithfully, in harmony with, and at peace with ourselves, we must recognize our own self-worth. We do not have to be the same as other people to be valued and loved. We can be true to the uniqueness of how we were created.

There is no one else like you in the world. Every person is different and has different experiences. Even twins, who may look just alike and may have the same DNA, will have different life experiences. It is amazing to look at the diversity in the world. That variation demonstrates a core principle: you have the right to be you because if you are not you, nobody will be you. What makes you unique does not exist anywhere else. Everybody has the right to be who they are, and we need to treat all people, each and every one of them, with that level of dignity and respect. Everyone has the right to love and be loved. Including you.

You have the right to love and be loved, as you are, for who you are. God created us to be connected to other humans: to have bonds with one another, to have unity, to be in family groups, to have friends, perhaps to be a significant other. God created all of that as a way for us to have joy and to have comfort, to love and be loved.

What does it mean to be loved? Perhaps the first question is to ask is what does the word 'love' mean? In English dictionaries, to feel love is described as 'to have a great interest and pleasure in something.' In English, we use that one word, 'love,' to mean many different concepts: I love my child, I love apples, I love the color green.

Here are four concepts from the Greek language that describe types of love:

- Eros – romantic, passionate love, from which we get our English word "erotic." Attraction based on sexual desire, affection, and tenderness felt by lovers.

- Storge – familial love, referring to natural or instinctual affection, such as the love of a parent toward offspring and children toward parents and siblings.

- Philia – the affectionate bond of friends, from which we get the name of the city "Philadelphia," the "city of brotherly love." It is about commitment, the love that binds one to another in enduring friendship, and strong affection for another.

- Agape – unconditional, self-sacrificing love that seeks the welfare of the other. Unselfish loyal and benevolent concern for the good of another, to do what is in the long-term best interest of another. Not just a feeling, but a choice of will.

We all have value and deserve to be loved

Humans have a core value just because they exist. Our value does not rely on anything we do or do not do, or on anything done to us. The value human beings have is simply because we exist. Think about a newborn baby, holding that tiny infant in your arms. Does that baby have value? Of course, it does. All that baby does is swallow and eliminate, but we understand that the baby has value just because they exist, just because they are human.

So, when does that baby lose its core value? When did you lose that inherent value you had as a baby? That is an unanswerable question because no one ever loses that value. Our inherent worth does not rely on anything that we do or not do or anything that happened to us or did not happen to us. We exist. We are valuable and worthy of dignity and respect, and nothing can destroy that value because we did not do anything to earn it.

In Summary

This is an important point and worth repeating: You are born with value and you never lose that basic value. There is nothing you can do to lose that value. Nothing that has happened to you can destroy that value. You do not have to be perfect to deserve love. No matter what anyone has said to you or about you, you are valuable, you are worthy. You have the right to love and be loved; to be cared about deeply and to care about others deeply.

CHAPTER TWO

You have the right to make mistakes, to be human – not perfect

We all make mistakes. Let me say that again, everybody makes mistakes. If somebody says they do not make mistakes, their most recent mistake is in thinking that they do not make mistakes. Making a mistake does not dimmish our core value as a human. It is normal and our right to make mistakes, often it is how we learn new things or make new discoveries. When we choose badly or incorrectly making an error or blunder in action, opinion, or judgment it is a mistake, an error caused by poor reasoning, carelessness, or inadequate knowledge. That is an action or decision that is wrong or produces a result that is not intended.

There are three different types of mistakes that we make.

- To willfully choose to disobey commands, to willfully break the law.
- To know what the good would be, but choose not to do it.
- To go astray, to miss the mark. Like an archer when shooting an arrow, but the arrow does not hit the bullseye. Something that just did not go quite right.

These are the most common kinds of mistakes.

God knows that we make mistakes and God knows that we do things that are wrong. Another way to describe these mistakes is the word 'sin.'

> *... for all have sinned and*
> *fall short of the glory of God,*
> *Romans 3:23*

We have the right to make mistakes, but we have the responsibility to handle what happens after a mistake in a healthy way. This is for our own benefit as well as for the benefit of others who may have been hurt because of our mistake. After the mistake, we have the choice of how to handle our mistakes. We can respond in a healthy way or handle our mistakes in an unhealthy way, thereby multiplying our mistakes.

When you make a mistake, own it, confess to it; do not blame, run, or hide. It is not so much what you did, as it is what you do after what you did, that may decide how bad a mistake will be. Don't waste your mistakes, learn from them! When you learn from other people's mistakes, you can get all the benefits without the pain.

> *"Been there,*
> *done that,*
> *Not doing that again!"*

It is not so much what you did, as it is what you do after what you did. You have a responsibility to deal with your mistakes and the after-effects. You can move forward to repair a mistake. Confession is the first step toward repairing a relationship. When you admit that you have done something wrong, that is a good start toward the repair. Working toward making whole, mending, or rebuilding, to put into good order something that is injured or damaged.

It is our right as human beings to make mistakes. We all do things that are wrong. We all have done things that that did not turn out well, where we have to restart and try again. Life's greatest lessons are often learned at the worst times and from the worst mistakes. Experience is simply the name we give our mistakes. However, remember that mistakes do not change our core value, our worth. A single mistake is not a change in direction; a single mistake is just a bump in the road that we can learn from. It does not define our character.

Sometimes we lose our way. We may do shameful things. We can focus on things that take us away from where we want to go. We can pursue a goal at the cost of relationships, or at the cost of our own integrity. We can deceive others; we can lie to ourselves. We may keep ourselves closed off from friends, we may make choices to be too open with untrustworthy people. We may see wrongs being done in front of us or even to us and we choose not to speak out. We may exercise poor judgment.

Forgiveness

Just because we make mistakes does not mean we have lost our value as humans. We are not lost forever. It is not our mistakes that define us. What matters are the choices we make after the mistakes. We can choose to accept responsibility for our own actions, agree with God about the wrong we did and choose to turn from that path and change our own behavior.

The key to learning from mistakes is to choose to admit your mistakes and make the changes you need in order to keep moving forward in your life. When you cannot admit your own mistakes, you stay stuck in them. God makes a way for us to repair mistakes with him. We can repent and turn from that way of life.

> *If we confess our sins, he is faithful and*
> *just and will forgive us our sins and*
> *purify us from all unrighteousness.*
> *1 John 1:9*

He offers us forgiveness and directs us to forgive others. Forgiveness is about goodness. It is about extending mercy to those who have harmed you, even if they do not deserve to be forgiven. There are two directions of forgiveness: giving forgiveness and receiving forgiveness. Choosing to give forgiveness is an active process, which includes a decision to let go of negative feelings or any thoughts of getting back at a person for the wrong they have done to you.

Receiving forgiveness means you have agreed with the other individual that you have done wrong and therefore you need forgiveness. God chooses to offer forgiveness to all who come to him confessing their wrongs and asking for forgiveness.

When we hold on to the mistakes of the past—our own and those done against us—we are hindered in our mind and in our emotions. It interferes with our ability to have good relationships. For healing these deep wounds, there is nothing as effective as forgiveness. Forgiving others brings strong benefits to the one who forgives. It can lower anxiety, decrease depression, and can have positive effects physically as well. Forgiving others can help you to move forward toward your own healing.

Forgiveness does not mean you have to put yourself at risk again with someone who has hurt you. You can choose to forgive while maintaining healthy boundaries. The choice to forgive can happen in a moment, but the process of forgiving can take time. The scars of old wounds you received may always be with you. But forgiveness can free you from the control of the person who hurt you and the bitterness that can erode the joy of your life.

Bear with each other and forgive one another if any of you has a grievance against someone.

Forgive as the Lord forgave you.
Colossians 3:13

In Summary

We all make mistakes, but our mistakes do not have to define us. Making a mistake does not dimmish our core value as a human. It is normal and our right to make mistakes, often it is how we learn new things or make new discoveries. Just because we make mistakes does not mean we are lost forever. It is not our mistakes that define us. What matters are the choices we make after the mistakes. We also have the responsibility to handle what happens after our mistakes in a healthy way. This is for our own benefit as well as for the benefit of others. We all need to forgive and be forgiven.

CHAPTER THREE

You have the right to say NO

You have the right to say 'No'. How do we know that we have the right to say 'No?' I can say with assurance that it is our God-given right to say 'No' – even to God himself. You get to make that choice. selecting or making a decision when you are faced with two or more possibilities. You are the one who judges, the merits of multiple options and choose what direction you will take.

> *... then choose for yourselves this day*
> *whom you will serve...*
> Joshua 24:15

When we say 'No,' there can be consequences, good or bad. When we say 'Yes,' there can be consequences, good or bad. If we say 'No' to things that bring trouble into our lives, life will be better. If you say 'Yes' to things that bring trouble into our lives, life will be worse. Consequences, the effect, result, or outcome of saying 'Yes' or 'No' may have negative results; we should weigh the cost.

If we cannot say "No", our "Yes" has little value. Our negative answer or decision, or expression of disagreement or refusing is a part of us exercising our freedom of choice. Our positive answer or expression of agreement or acceptance only has value when we have the power to say no.

When somebody is in an abusive relationship, the abuser will tell them that they do not have the right to say 'No.' "You cannot say no to this." "You cannot say no to me." Those words are backed up by force, intimidation, or manipulation. When a child is forced it is driven into them that they cannot say 'No,' not even to how or when their body being touched, it damages a child's ability to trust the world. When a child is sexually abused, the damage inside of that child will take a lot to heal. As an adult, they may find it hard to tell people 'No.' Perhaps you can't say 'No' to the boss who is asking you if you could work an extra two hours tonight, even though you had things you needed to do after work and you were so tired. Maybe you do not feel like you can risk saying 'No.' When friends say, let us go to this place or let us go do that, you think it is too dangerous to say 'No' even though you do not want to go. If you say 'No' you fear you might lose your friendship, you might lose the job. The lingering effects of childhood abuse can greatly affect an adult. When we have been abused and traumatized as children, it makes it hard for us to say 'No' to anybody.

When we say 'No,' we might say it tentatively, like, 'I do not think I really want to do that,' or 'I do not really know,' or 'I would rather not.' Rather than just coming up with a calm and assertive 'No, that is not going to work for me.' Instead, the attitude comes out as 'No but please do not be mad at me because I said no, and you could actually talk me into it if you if you try.' Was that really a 'No'? Did you feel like you had the power to say 'No'? It can be good to look around in your life where you say, 'Yes' and where you say 'No.' Do you need to work on your clear, assertive, and polite delivery?

If it feels uncomfortable to say 'No,' practice saying 'No' to things where it does not matter and there is no perceived cost for you. For instance, say 'No' about watching that TV show, or going for a walk, or strawberry ice cream. It lets you hear yourself say a calm, assertive 'No,' and not feel any negative consequences for it. That will help you to learn how to be more assertive in places where it might be a little riskier to say 'No.'

When saying 'No' you do not have to yell. You do not have to be mad. You do not have to say it in an angry way. 'No' is an entire sentence. No. You do not have to say anything else with it. You can say 'No, thank you,' or you can say 'No, that will not work for me,' but 'No' is enough. When you say 'No' and give an explanation, like, 'Well, that will not work because I have this other thing I have to do,' you are inviting other people to fix that problem for you: 'Well, you could actually do that later and do my thing now.' When you give somebody a 'No,' you do not have to explain why. You do not have to invite them to change your mind for you.

When I am teaching a workshop sometimes people ask me if they can ask me a question. My response is always 'Sure you can ask me anything.' And before they have a chance to ask me, I say

- 'The answer to some things is yes.'

- 'The answer to some things is no.'

- 'The answer to some stuff is I don't know.'

And the answer to some stuff is 'That is information I choose not to share."

And when I say to someone 'That is information, I choose not to share.' I am not lying, I am not distracting, I am not hiding or manipulating. I am just clear and straightforward that that is information I choose not to share. And they might even ask me "Why not?" and the answer is "That is information I also choose not to share." And then I go on with another part of the conversation.

If somebody constantly is badgering me about why and they will not leave it alone, then I just end the conversation. I am done. I stated what my position is on it. I stated it politely. If I stay part of that conversation there are only other two other ways to go. Either I am going to escalate because I am getting irritated, or I am going to give in to what they want when I already know it is not in the best interest to do that. So instead of giving in or getting angry, I am just going to end that conversation.

Especially easy when you are on the phone. The thing about the phone is it disconnects from your end as well as the other end. I never hang up on anybody. I will always say goodbye. Now the thing is, they may not be through talking to me and they might be talking over me. I may have to talk over them, politely, and say "I am through with this conversation now." "I am going to hang up now.' 'Goodbye." I am being polite; I am being respectful, and I am leaving the conversation before I have to get irritated and escalate my volume and tone. And if they call right back, I will let it go to voicemail.

If I am texting, I do the same. I politely say this is my last text about this topic. I am going to end our conversation now. Goodbye. And I do not respond to any other texts about it.

Clean Communication

When you say 'Yes' to something, do you give a clear yes? Perhaps somebody asks you a question; do you say "Well, maybe,' or 'that might be OK"? Clean communication is a plain 'Yes.' When you can give a clear yes and a clear no, it makes life and relationships a lot easier for other people to interact with you. They do not have to wonder what you mean. You do not have to be angry someone asked you something you do not want to do, when you can just calmly and assertively say 'Yes' or 'No.' No explanations needed.

In summary

You have the right to say "No." If you cannot say "No", your "Yes" has little value. "No" is a complete sentence and you do not have to make excuses or explain. When you are asked why you can say 'That is information, I choose not to share.' In a calm, firm manner you can be clear and straightforward that your no means no.

CHAPTER FOUR

You have the right to choose your own values and beliefs

Values are like fingerprints.
Nobody's are the same,
but you leave 'em all over everything you do.
— Elvis Presley

Values and beliefs

Our first values and beliefs were handed to us from the important adults in our lives: parents or neighbors or extended family members or teachers. We also took them in from the media we watch, what we read, and things we learn. From a young age, we looked around our world and tried to make sense of it. Our first values and beliefs are unconsciously developed through these many sources. They are how we determined what was important to us, the principles that helped us to decide what was useful and right. As we mature, we evaluate what we see and what we hear, and what we experience around us.

Values have a major influence on our behaviors and attitudes and serve us as broad guidelines in choosing what actions are best to do or what way is best to live. We assess whether what we see is good or bad, beneficial or harmful. We make decisions about what we will agree or disagree with. We decide what to believe, have faith or confidence in someone or something. Our beliefs are firmly held opinions or convictions. As adults, we take responsibility for and ownership of our own values and beliefs.

To illustrate, imagine I am walking along a nature area. Acres and acres of woods and fields. On the pathway up ahead, I see in the dappled shade a big S shape. That is neutral information, but I have an adrenaline reaction. I am not reacting to the neutral information of an S shape in the path. My instant adrenaline reaction is in response to the beliefs and values of my childhood. I think: S shape is a snake, all snakes are venomous, all snakes bite people, all people bitten by venomous snakes die horribly.

These are the beliefs developed in my childhood. My accompanying value is that I want to be safe, and living is better than dying.

Now if these are my beliefs and values, it would make sense to run away and never go there again. And my world would get smaller. But I also have other values: I value truth and the courage to face hard things. As a maturing adult, I am willing to examine this more closely. So, I see that shape like an S up ahead on the pathway. Neutral information. I feel an adrenaline reaction. This is also a neutral observation. I could ask myself, "What is the truth about what is going on here?"

While my instant adrenaline response is to think it is a snake, it could be a snake, could be a tree root, could be a vine, could be an old piece of rope. Truth is, I do not have enough information to assess it at this distance.

My adrenaline response to think all snakes are venomous. Truth is, some snakes are venomous, most are not. According to National Geographic, there are more than 3,000 species of snakes on the planet. About 600 species are venomous, and only about 200—seven percent—are able to kill or significantly wound a human. In the part of the world I live in, there are NO native venomous snakes. Truth is, even if it is a snake, it is not likely to be venomous.

My adrenaline response is to think all snakes bite people. Truth is that snakes do not bite people unless they feel threatened. The main purpose of snake venom has to do with the prey they kill and eat. I am too big for a venomous snake to eat.

My adrenaline response is to think all people bitten by venomous snakes die horribly. Truth is, according to the Centers for Disease Control, out of a population of over 325 million Americans, only 7,000–8,000 people per year receive venomous snake bites in the

United States, and only about five of those people die. I live in a part of the world with good medical care.

Having examined the truth, I get to choose my next action. I choose to cautiously continue down the trail to get a closer look. I see it is a tree root and I go on with my walk. I have exercised my courage and I did not make my world smaller. My behavior was driven by my values and beliefs.

My instant adrenaline response was created in childhood. I was raised by a mother who was hysterically afraid of snakes. She would not even look at a picture of a snake in a book. As a child, you get your information about danger and safety from the adults around you. At three years old, if you see your mom see a snake and she gets hysterical about it, you figure there is a danger there. If the adult in your life cannot handle the danger then of course it must be a really bad danger, which can put a deep trauma imprint on a child. Fortunately, I also had a dad who was matter-of-fact about snakes. So, although I had the instant adrenaline response, my mind would say it is not a big deal, a sort of balancing act in my mind and body.

As a parent, I decided to raise my child not to be afraid of snakes. I would catch a little garden snake to show him what it was like and let him touch it and then we let it go. We would go to the reptile exhibits at the zoo, where there were large snakes to look at and touch. I was intentional about exposing him calmly to snakes because I did not want him to catch that fearful adrenaline response from his grandmother. Even now when I see a snake I still have a small adrenaline flash because of that early childhood imprinting, but my mind has already decided that the adrenaline flash is not accurate and therefore I just cautiously analyze what is going on around me and go on with my day.

Values inform our behavior

My parents were born at the beginning of the Great Depression, and the attitude then was "use it up, wear it out, make do or do without." And so, the habit of my parents was to gather stuff. Stuff was rare and precious and therefore needed to be gathered and collected and held onto. I'm not talking about a bunch of heritage antiques here. I'm talking about 75 empty plastic yogurt containers. I grew up in a house where you had to turn sideways to go down the hall because of the stuff. We moved a lot and we lived in trailers and small houses, and clutter always surrounded us because they hung on to the values their parents gave them about stuff is rare and precious and therefore must be collected and hung on to because you may need it and will not be able to get it.

Now I live in a house that's fairly empty, fairly simple, and a balanced minimalist. Yet I am still honoring the values of my parents. I believe what is rare and precious needs to be collected and taken care of so you will have it when you need it. To my parents, that was stuff. To me, it is time, open space, and calmness. Stuff steals those things. While I am still honoring the value I was raised with, the way I express it is totally different.

27

In my counseling practice, when people talk about needing more stuff, I suggest they go into any neighborhood in June, which is garage sale season in my part of the world, when people sell off their extra stuff. Show up on Sunday at about 3 o'clock in the afternoon. You can ask those people at the end of a weekend selling things if there is anything they are giving away. I doubt you will get 10 blocks before your vehicle is overflowing. The sellers don't want to put the stuff back in their garage again. To give it away is a relief. Where I live, in the United States, there is an overabundance of stuff. Secondhand stores are full of stuff. There is stuff given away on social media. Stuff is neither rare nor precious here. What is precious are time and empty space.

If I pick up that free stuff and bring it to my house, pretty soon my house would be so full you'd have to turn sideways to walk down the hall. Soon I would not even know what I have because I do not have time to use it or look at it. My home would then look like my parents' home. But I would not be honoring the core of the values I grew up with.

I like to have enough stuff to know I have what I need when I need it. Other stuff I want to send on and let other people be blessed by it. I have to be diligent, so stuff doesn't take over my world and clutter doesn't take over my life. There is a point at which we no longer own stuff; stuff starts to own us. Decluttering is a regular part of my life. I donate stuff three or four times a year. Calmness is precious to me and calmness does not thrive in a place that's cluttered.

*"It's not hard to make decisions
when you know what your values are."*
— *Roy Disney*

Aspirational values and behavioral values

Another facet of values and beliefs is the difference between aspirational values and behavioral values. An important value of mine is to eat healthily and to have a strong body in good condition. But I can struggle with this. If I am overweight, my behavioral value may be that "I want what I want when I want it." It does not mean that my aspirational value is not my value. It just means it is an area in which I struggle. But it is helpful to take a look at the difference between your aspirational values—the things you say are important—and your behavioral values—the things that you do—and see if those lineup.

What does the way you spend your money say about your values? Are the things you spend money on in line with your values? Or are your behavioral values with money closer to "I want what I want when I want it"? What does the way you spend your time say about your values? If you say people are important to you, but you spend all your time at work and not with the people you say are important, what does that tell others about your values? You might say "I am working for my family so they can have stuff they need." But how much stuff is really needed? Where is the balance?

In Summary

You were handed a set of values when you were young, and you took them in from the people around you, the world around you, and how you understood them. But as you get older and mature you have the ability to look at those values and examine them and decide are these really my values? Do I really agree with these? What do my behaviors say about these values? You get to choose, and you have the power to change your values and beliefs.

CHAPTER FIVE

You have the right to your own feelings and opinions and to express them

You are the expert

Y ou are the expert on your feelings, your emotional state, and your own opinions. You are the one who knows about you. No one else has your background or can see inside of you. No one else can tell you what you feel.

Feelings and emotions

Feelings are something experienced through touch or emotion. Feelings result from emotional responses or tendencies to respond, sentiments, or desires. Feelings vary depending upon one's tendency to handle a situation, how the situation relates to past experiences, and any number of other factors. Feelings are the conscious experience of emotional reactions.

Our feelings tend to follow our thinking. Feelings can just flash up; they can be triggered, and they are just there. But when they do arrive, we can add intensity to them, or we can take intensity away from them and calm them down. Our emotions are a natural instinctive state of mind deriving from our circumstances, mood, or relationships with others. Emotions can be affected by our past experiences and may not accurately reflect present circumstances.

Sometimes people have a hard time putting a name to their feeling. It may not be because they do not know what they are feeling, but rather because they do not have the feeling vocabulary to accurately identify and name the feeling.

Free resource to help develop and expand your feeling words vocabulary with over 24 feeling faces and over 500 words that describe feelings.

www.FaithfulHabits.com/Fundamentals

Our feelings give us information, but that information is influenced by the way we think. It is influenced by our experience, our worldview, and the way, we grew up. When we have a strong feeling about something, it is good to stop and look at why the feeling is so strong.

If you were sitting in a crowded room and somebody across the room is staring right at you with a puzzled, scowling, negative look on their face, you might think they were scowling at you. You look down at yourself and wonder, are they judging what I am wearing? Do they not like how I combed my hair? Do they hate me? We make up a story for ourselves about what is going on. Perhaps we decide the person is being disrespectful and they do not like me, or that person doesn't like the clothes I'm wearing, or they think I dress funny. We can make up this whole story in our own head, usually a negative one, about what's going on. Then our emotions flare up and we can begin to get angry about it. We think, "How dare they judge me like that!"

But on the other side of the room, that person is lost in thought. They do not even see you because they aren't sure whether they left the iron plugged in when they left home and they are worried that they may burn their house down. You just happen to be in their line of sight for that moment; their expression has absolutely nothing to do with you. You got yourself in a heightened emotional state when it was all in your own head. Their facial expression and their thoughts had nothing to do with you.

That is an example of how we can have a strong feeling, but the feeling is not accurate. If you react out of that feeling, venting your frustration and anger on that person, you are the one in the wrong. What would that incident look like from the other side? The person is minding their own business, trying to remember if they left the iron plugged in at home, when someone comes over and, without any reason or warning, starts yelling at them. They will likely react to the perceived danger of an unprovoked attack and you can be in a pretty intense argument. Over nothing.

A way to prevent this type of conflict is to assume the best intentions from other people. Pause to ask questions and get more information. We have the right to feel what we're feeling, and no one else can tell us what we're feeling, but our rights end where another person's rights begin. We do not always have the right to act on those feelings, and we have the responsibility to check our feelings before we use them as a reason to cause conflict or trouble with others. Our feelings give us information, but not always accurate information. We use our feeling to inform our opinions. But if our feelings are not accurate, our strongly held opinions also may not always be accurate.

Opinions

Our opinions are a view, belief, attitude, or judgment we have formed; an estimation of the quality or worth of someone or something—not necessarily based on fact or knowledge, not necessarily accurate—but generally believed to be accurate by the opinion-holder. People often have an emotional reaction to opinions, or they can state their opinions intensely.

When somebody says, "I am always right," the first thing we may think is that it sounds like an arrogant statement. But think about it for a moment. You may be just as likely to think you are always right. Why would anyone hold an opinion they think is wrong? If I hold an opinion and you convince me that my opinion is wrong, I will change my opinion and then I am right again. It is likely that everybody thinks they are always right; they have the accurate opinion. That they are free from error or defect in thinking. They think their opinions are consistent with what is right.

People have strongly held opinions about what is right or wrong in things as simple as how food should be flavored or eaten; and about things as complex and important as what are the rights of a group of people in what situation and why. Many of these opinions are in direct opposition to other people's opinions. How do we know what is accurate, who is right or wrong?

Accurate

When it is not accurate, it is wrong; it breaks some standard. When we say something is wrong, not correct or true, a question to ask ourselves is "Wrong according to what standard?"

- Is it wrong according to a legal standard?
- Is it wrong according to a moral standard?
- Is it wrong according to a biblical standard?
- Is it wrong according to an ethical standard? Which ethical standard?
- Is it wrong according to a standard of competency?
- Is it wrong according to a personal preference standard?

For example, if the window glass gets washed and it has streaks all over it, we would say that the window was washed wrong. But it is not illegal to leave streaks on a window. It is not immoral to leave streaks on the glass. The Bible does not discuss the washing of window glass. It is not unethical to leave streaks on the glass. But according to the professional competency standards of window washing, leaving streaks is wrong. And perhaps it is also wrong according to personal preference.

So, when we say something is wrong, it is good to stop and think: wrong according to what standard? Sometimes when we state something is wrong, we are stating our own personal preference standard. If I say all walls should be painted off-white and you say some walls should have vibrant color, neither of us is wrong, and neither of us is right. It is a matter of personal choice. It is not illegal, it is not immoral, nothing is in scripture to decide it, it breaks no ethical standard, and it is not even a competency issue. Where it can become wrong is if we try to force our personal preference into areas that are not our responsibility, when we are trying to tell other people what to do with their own decisions.

While we have the right to our own feelings, emotions, and opinions we need to remember that everyone else also has this right. They may not agree with us. That is okay; that is their right.

In Summary

You have the right to your own feelings, emotions, and opinions and to express them. But you do not have the right for everyone to agree with you. We have the right to feel what we're feeling, and no one else can tell us what we're feeling, but our rights end where another person's begin. We have the responsibility to check our feelings before we use them as a reason to cause conflict or trouble with others. If our feelings are not accurate, our strongly held opinions also may not always be accurate. When we think something is wrong, it is good to stop and ask, "wrong according to what standard?" Everyone else also has a right to their own feelings and opinions and to express them.

CHAPTER SIX

You have the right to change
your mind and your life

It is common to think of change as uncomfortable. It takes effort, it may feel unfamiliar. But unfamiliar is not the same as wrong, nor the same as uncomfortable. It just means you have not done it this way before. So the more appropriate word may be "unfamiliar." Try a little exercise: Put your hands together, fingers interlaced. Do it again faster and once more even faster. Now, look at which thumb is on top. Now, put your hands together again, with the other thumb on top. Do it again, faster. Was that easy? Did it feel unfamiliar? Did it take intentional effort? That was only a tiny change, too. So, when changing bigger things, expect to put in some effort.

You have the right to change your life,
and you have the ability to change your life.

Change is all around us. In fact, anything that is alive grows. Anything that grows, changes. Anything that is not growing is declining. Children grow and change almost before our eyes. Trees and plants in the garden are constantly in the process of changing. Any product you bought new is aging and wearing out. Some changes are slow, and others are fast. Change is a natural part of life, and change can be amazing.

Every day we reinforce habits in our life. Are they the negative habits that make life harder or are they positive habits that make life better? We get to make that choice every day. In every big choice, there are many small choices. These little choices add to the pleasure or the misery in our life. You have the power to examine your life. You get to assess what is already helpful and what needs to be strengthened. You also get to assess what is making your life harder and what needs to be totally changed.

You have the power to examine your life and to change your life

To change is to become different; to start something new. It can be exciting to learn something new. Think about a time when you felt the excitement of getting something new or learning something new. Remember that exciting feeling as you think about changing a habit. Try to cultivate it even over something small. Change takes time and effort. The good news is that you have the power to make changes in your life to make your life better.

A habit is the tendency to act in a particular way, something that you do often and regularly, sometimes without knowing that you are doing it. Every one of us has hundreds of habits we use regularly that make life go easier. The way you comb your hair, the way you brush your teeth, the way you reach to turn on a light in a dark room: all of these are habits. Making a new habit will take making a vigorous or determined effort, but the result will save you a lot of effort moving forward. There is an intentional process in the effort to make a new habit.

When you are learning how to ride a bike, there is a lot to remember: the way to push the pedal, where to hang on to the handlebars, how much to turn the handlebars so make a right turn without falling down, how to balance to keep the bike upright, which side of the road to ride on, what the road signs mean. Oh, and where are you going?

When you learn a new skill, there are many steps to each task. It is a lot to think about all at once, so you take the time to develop good habits for each skill. Later, those habits help you to not have to pay much attention to those details anymore, you just automatically do it. In the same way, changing your life is a process of changing habits. Habits are, by definition, strongly held actions in our lives. Therefore, it is easier to replace a habit than it is to stop a habit. Instead of only saying you will watch less TV, when you get home from work, you pick up your running shoes instead of the remote. So, replacing one habit with a different habit is better and healthier for your life. Sometimes you can shift a habit just a little bit to bring it toward a healthy place.

The way to determine which habits to change, or which new habits to develop, is to examine your life. Think about areas in your life that are uncomfortable. Examine things that seem harder than they should be; inspect in detail to determine their nature or condition; investigate thoroughly. When you take the time to examine hard places in your life, you can often think of new ways to make your life easier. Just because you have always done it that way does not mean you have to do it that way in the future.

You are not trapped by your past; you can make changes. You can change your actions, and you can change your reputation. You do not have to be in the future what you were in the past. People who have not met you yet do not know your reputation. You are free to change it by learning a new skill or practicing new behaviors. People you have not met yet will only know you by the new reputation you build. You get to choose. What do you want your reputation to be?

You have the power to look at your beliefs, your values, your feelings, your opinions, and your emotions. Examine them for what is true and accurate. You get to choose what is important to you. Expect that putting the choice into practice will take effort and your emotions and feelings will lag behind your choices.

One of the easiest times I have found to change a habit is when I move to a new home. Everything is in a different place; I have to make a bunch of new habits anyway, so if I put a little thought into how I will shift my habits, I can move toward a healthier life.

In summary

You have the right and the power to change your life. Change can feel unfamiliar but that is not the same as wrong, nor the same as uncomfortable. Change is all around us. Change is a natural part of life, and change can be amazing. We make choices each day to keep doing things the same way or to make changes. These choices add to the pleasure or the misery in our life. You can change your habit, actions, and reputation. You get to choose what your future will be like.

PART TWO

RELATIONAL FUNDAMENTALS

Relational rights are the rights that we have as we relate to other people: family, friends, bosses, children, parents, neighbors, a significant other, and all the different people that we interact with life. Relational rights provide healthy ways for people to interact while respecting each other's dignity and rights.

- You have the right to be safe, to be treated with dignity and respect.
- You have the right to healthy friendships.
- You have the right to choose when and how your body is touched.
- You have the right to treat yourself as well as you treat others.
- You have the right not to be responsible for other adults' choices, feelings, and behavior.
- You have the right to feel angry and leave if you are treated abusively.

This part of the book will expand on each of the rights above, exploring how we live out these rights, to help you to understand your relational rights as a human being. Also providing a road map of how you can respect these rights for yourself and respect these rights for others.

CHAPTER SEVEN

You have the right to be safe, to be treated with dignity and respect

You have the right to safety in relationships

There is safety in relationships when we are connected in ways that are beneficial to all parties. Everyone benefits and life runs more smoothly; people are protected from potential harm, danger, risk, or injury. We have the right to be treated with dignity and respect. Dignity is the inherent and equal value and worth everyone is born with. Respect is polite behavior, treating people in a positive manner that acknowledges them for who they are and/or what they are doing. Treating people with dignity and respect is a part of safe, healthy behavior in relationships.

Safety in all relationships, not just romantic ones

Often, when we think about relationships, we may focus on the most connected of all relationships, which is the connection to that one special someone, our significant other. But that is only one possible relationship of many that we have. We also have relationships with our children, other family, adult children, parents, siblings. and more family with cousins, in-laws, aunts and uncles, grandparents, etc. Those are only the family relationships.

Relationships are the way in which people are connected, the way in which people regard and behave toward each other. We also have relationships with friends, acquaintances, neighbors, landlord, employer, coworkers, people at school, people who provide services, people who work in stores, and many others. If all those relationships are safe, they can be wonderful. They add richness and value to our lives.

A safe relationship

Safe relationships look different among different people we have connections with. We have the right to safety in relationships and to protect ourselves from unsafe relationships and the occasional unsafe behaviors within otherwise safe relationships.

Examples of mutually beneficial relationships:

- **Friends** – A give and take, enjoying each other's company, respecting each other's time and other commitments. Being able to share information and not be gossiped about.

- **Neighbors** – Politeness and respecting each other's space and property. Respecting each other's right to quiet enjoyment.

- **Our landlord** – Respecting the landlord's property, taking reasonable care of what you have rented. Landlord respecting tenant's right to quiet enjoyment, providing a livable space.

- **Our boss** – Receiving value towards a goal of business, an employee receiving wages for work done. Both are respectful.

- **Coworkers** – Polite, respectful, helpful working relationship as you move toward common goals.

- **With the people at school** – being able to rely on the school providing education and the school being able to rely on students attending and fulfilling responsibilities.

These relationships are safe if they work well, with each person receiving benefit and their lives being made easier and calmer. There is a sense of kindly being together and enjoying their time together.

Unsafe interactions

When these relationships have unsafe interactions, either being rude, aggressive, deceptive, or abusive, the ability to trust is broken, and life becomes more stressful. Relationships are unsafe if one person is behaving in a way that is beneficial only to themselves and may create damage, struggle, discomfort, loss, pain, and uncertainty into the lives of others.

When an offense or damage is caused by unsafe behavior, the appropriate remedy is to confront the offender in a polite, respectful but firm manner. If you cannot get the concern resolved, then it is time to take the concern to a higher authority, with a couple of other witnesses, or a supervisor, or some other legal remedy. You do not have to resort to unsafe behaviors in return to try to get your concern taken care of.

Safe behaviors enrich relationships

With family and friends, safety in relationships is where somebody respects you and treats you with dignity. They see your value as important as their own. They want to help, encourage, and support you to grow into who you can be in your own special uniqueness. In safe relationships, someone listens to you; they pay attention to your opinions and your feelings. Even when you do not agree, you can still be civil and respectful of the person. It is where you pay attention to their feelings and opinions. You respect them and treat them with dignity, and you see their value as much as your own. There is equality in the relationship.

People with safe behaviors encourage you to be the best you can be. They do not tear you down with unkind words. When they want something from you, they straightforwardly ask for it. You are free to answer yes or no. If you say yes, they are grateful for that, and if you say no, they accept your no, and it does not affect your relationship.

Unsafe behaviors are different.

Unsafe behaviors can be slightly annoying, or they can be damaging or abusive. Abusive behavior is the improper use of something or someone; to use to bad effect or for a bad purpose; to misuse; to treat with cruelty or violence, especially regularly or repeatedly. Any action that intentionally harms or injures another person in any way is committing abuse. When a truly abusive situation exists, it is because one party is seeking to control the other through coercion or intimidation. It is as if the one person is saying, "I want what I want and I do not care what the effect of that is on you."

Family counseling with a mental health professional can help a family move away from unsafe behaviors and learn how to be in safe relationships with each other. However, when someone refuses to change unsafe behaviors or get help, the only way to break the cycle may be to leave the relationship.

All forms of abuse are illegal in the United States: physical abuse, emotional abuse, spiritual abuse, verbal abuse, sexual abuse, mental abuse, and financial abuse.

Everyone has the right to be safe in relationships.

In significant other relationships, there is a common pattern in the abuse cycle. At first, everything is going great, and the couple is getting along fine. The abuser and the victim are in a comfortable, happy state. Then tension builds. The victim feels like they are walking on eggshells. They have a sense of uneasiness, feeling like abuse is likely to happen at any moment. Then the abuse happens and, whether it is physical, emotional, or sexual abuse, the victim is hurt and in pain. Afterward, the abuser may seem sorry or even apologize. This seems like remorse and the abuser may say, "I did not mean to do that." They may even say, "It will never happen again." Or the abuser may blame the victim. "I would not have done that if you had not done what you did." "You caused me to do this." At this point, there may be a period of peace or calm or even the appearance of happiness where everything seems to be going wonderfully. The abuser is loving and caring. Then the happiness starts to fade away and the tension builds again, and it is back into the cycle of abuse. This will be discussed more in chapter twelve.

Everyone has behaved unsafely at times

We need to understand that all of us at one time or another have behaved unsafely toward someone else. Whether intentionally or carelessly, we have all done something that was in our own interest and negatively affected others. That is common. But not everyone has behaved abusively. That is NOT a common behavior. Unsafe behaviors are often learned in the environment in which somebody grows up and it is what they understood as the way things worked in the world, and so they repeat that way of interacting with others. But unsafe behaviors can be unlearned, and new, safe behaviors can be learned, making life better for everybody. We can ask for forgiveness for our behavior and give grace to others as well.

In summary

We all deserve to have safety in relationships, to be treated with dignity and respect. We have many different kinds of relationships in our lives, and in each relationship, there can be safe and unsafe behaviors. When there are unsafe behaviors, we may need to remind people of our boundaries, that we are to be treated with respect. We need to be intentional to treat others with respect. If others choose not to treat us with respect, we can evaluate our options of confronting them or removing ourselves from the closeness of that relationship.

CHAPTER EIGHT

You have the right to heathy friendships

Friendships

Friends are an important part of a healthy life. We all need people we can talk with, friends that we know and who knows us, a mutual bond of like and trust. Wise friends question, encourage, coach, and challenge each other. A close friend has your long-term best interest at heart. We all need a number of friends at different levels of closeness in our lives.

There are many levels of friendship:

We meet people as strangers and over time we can grow into a friendly relationship with a lot of people. Different levels of friendship include casual friends, good friends, and friends with which you have a close and deep bond.

- The very best of friends, the ones I want as a meaningful part of my life, are three or four really close friends. These are people who know me well and support and encourage me. They are people I can turn to when I am in trouble and they will help me. I share my joys with them, and they delight in my happiness. We talk and meet regularly.

- The next level of friendship is a good friend. These I may have about a dozen of. We make time for each other; we go to events together and share meals together. Every month we make time for each other and enjoy each other's company.

- Now we come to casual friends. These are people I enjoy the company of when I am with them, but I do not go out of my way to make time for them, and they do not make time for me. When we are together, we are friends. These could be co-workers, or people I talk with every year at a specific event, or people I chat with every Sunday morning at church.

- Next are friendly acquaintances. These include the worker at the grocery store I have been going to for ten years, or the librarian where I borrow books, people I greet casually Sunday morning as I walk by, etc. People I am around on a regular basis, but I do not truly know them, and they do not truly know me.

- Now we come to familiar faces. These are people I do not know, but I recognize that I see them regularly: perhaps the person who walks their dog in my neighborhood, or the person at the bus stop each weekday. I do not know them. They do not know me. But they seem to belong in my world.

- Everyone else is a stranger.

How we make friends

To make friends, I look around my world for a friendly face, perhaps a familiar face I have often seen before. I make eye contact for a moment to see if they look interested. Then I make a statement about neutral shared experience: the weather, or something interesting or beautiful around us. Small talk invites them to talk with me. As we share small talk I am asking myself –'Is this someone I like? Would I like to know more about them?' Small talk has a low commitment level I can end the conversation at any time.

From the small talk, we can venture into a little about ourselves or our general interests: whether we have a dog, how our dog likes to play. However, we stay public and general in our conversation, taking time to get to know a little about this person, see if they are someone we might like to get to know better. This may take a few more meetings.

If this is someone we decide we want to get to know better, we can ask more about their life and see if they would like to learn more about your life. Ideally, this becomes a back and forth of sharing more and slightly deeper conversation about interests.

Over time, conversations become more about our beliefs, opinions, values, and the things we hold dear. We share this little by little and see what they do with it. Going too deep too soon may make you vulnerable to someone who is not safe, or it may scare the other person off because they feel too vulnerable, and they do not yet know if you are safe. Take your time. The goal is a long-term friendship that you can deeply share. No rush.

Ways to have a good conversation

Good conversations can be like swimming. We spend time swimming on the surface, then we take a deep breath and dive down deep to experience the treasures and beauty below. After some time underwater, we come up for air so we can go down again. Small talk is our first toe in the water. It is a greeting that makes a statement and asks an important question: "I am a friendly human being. Are you a friendly human being?" We do not actually say that, though. Instead, we do weather talk, or sports talk, or other neutral shared experiences. "It is hot today." Or "The clouds are thick this morning." The purpose of neutral small talk is to invite the other person to talk. If I state an opinion like, "I hate how hot it is today," or "I love how hot it is," I am not inviting someone to talk to me, I am only looking for an audience, so I can state my own views. By phrasing my comment neutrally, like, "It is hot today," I invite the other person to state their opinion about the topic. I am inviting conversation by demonstrating that I am a friendly person willing to have a mutual conversation. Small talk is a good way to start conversations, and when conversations do go deep, it is good to have a moment to lower the intensity and come up for air.

The purpose of 'small talk'

Some people do not want to spend time talking the small talk. They want to have deep conversations about important topics from the first meeting. Trouble is that those people may have difficulty finding close friends. Other people seem to spend all their time in only small talk and rarely if ever talk about deeper things. When someone brings up a deeper topic they get uncomfortable. They may have many friends, but few if any close friends.

Making close friends takes a balance of small talk and deeper talk. We tend to be drawn toward those who are most comfortable at the depth of conversations we are comfortable with. Being able to politely engage in small talk, at least for a while, or being able to endure deeper talk for a while will help you find those who want to grow closer. It takes time and effort to develop a rich friend network. In order to have friends, one must be friendly.

Eye contact as a component of conversation.

The amount of appropriate eye contact in a conversation can vary some culture to culture. How much is too much? How little is too little? In my culture, constant eye contact is usually a part of deep intimacy or aggressive behavior, a threat. No eye contact can be seen as rude, disregarding, or ignoring

61

behavior. Polite eye contact is to look into someone's eyes while they are talking, showing that you are paying attention. After a moment or two, break eye contact to look down or glance away, then look back again. That shows a respectful, friendly attentiveness. Too much staring can feel too intense and make the other person feel uncomfortable. Too little eye contact can feel like the person is bored and make the other person feel uncomfortable. Some people prefer less eye contact some prefer more. Good conversation is an art form.

Distance apart when talking

The comfortable distance apart that people stand or sit while having a conversation varies from culture to culture. In my culture, it is comfortable to stand a little more than the length of my arm away from the person I am talking to. To stand closer would be perhaps appropriate if the environment is noisy and I am trying to hear, but generally, closer is appropriate to share more of a sense of intimacy or express an aggressive threat. To stand much farther apart would be to express disinterest. Seeking to find the appropriate distance apart in conversation makes people more comfortable together. Standing or sitting too close can feel like an aggressive demand of intimacy without consent.

The characteristics of good friends

A good friend is safe. They will never use anything they know about you to hurt you. They are honest; they do not lie to you or deceive you. They encourage you to be the best you can be. They do not want to lead you into behaviors that will hurt you or that are against your integrity. They speak the truth to you. They are kind and gentle. They are fun. They do not make fun of you or shame you or try to embarrass you. They speak well of you to others. They speak well of others to you. They do not try to dominate your time. They understand that you have other people in your life that are a higher priority than they are, and they do not take offense when you cannot spend time with them.

A good friend is loyal to you, you can trust them to have your long-term best interest at heart. Someone who is faithful to one's oath, commitments, or obligations. Truth is in your best interest. That means a good friend is more loyal to the truth than they are to you. A good friend will not lie to you, nor will they lie for you. As a good friend, you would not ask them to lie for you. A good friend will not ask you to do something against your own values. A faithful friend is more committed to what is right than they are committed to you. It is not in your long-term best interest to do wrong, therefore a good friend faithfully helps you to do what is right and helps you to think through your choices in line with your values. They are consistent and reliable; they are true to their word. Someone you can depend on to do what is right.

Friends vs Using Buddies

Sometimes people think they have friends, but what they have is people who are only friendly with you when there is some benefit to themselves, like a person who you share a resource with but is only with you when you have some of the resources to give them. They want you to share your resources with them, but they make no effort to share with you. They frequently contact you for help and support when life is hard for them. But they don't have time to help and support you when you are stressed.

They want your encouragement, but they don't encourage you. Your time together is generally about them and their needs. Also, they may be quick to criticize you, how you dress, friends you have, things you do. They behave as if their opinions are the only right opinions. They may speak disrespectfully of other people, gossiping and spreading rumors.

These kinds of behaviors do not fit on any level of a healthy friend; they may just be a "using buddy." Basically, they are only friendly with you when they can use you or your resources.

A Significant Other

Happiness is being married to your best friend. As we search for that one special person to share our life with, social proof is a good step along that process. Go with this person to meet with their friends and family. How do they behave around their family and friends? How do their family and friends treat them? What seems to be their reputation with these people?

Take them to meet your family and friends. Let them see how you act around the people you are the most comfortable with. Let them see how you respond to various people who know your history and are a part of your current life. You will learn a lot about each other during this process. If they do not want to share that part of their life with you, that tells you something important about this person. What is hidden? Why is it hidden? Are they ashamed of you? Are they ashamed of where they come from? Why do they not have friends? These are important questions. As you seek to know more of someone who may become your significant other you grow more in shared intimacy with each other.

Areas of intimacy

When we discuss intimacy, many people think of just one kind of intimacy – sexual intimacy. However, there are many different kinds of intimacy:

- **Social Intimacy** – Sharing our friends with our friends, getting to know the friends of our friends.

- **Sexual Intimacy** – Sharing a faithful sexual relationship, a sexual bond.

- **Physical Intimacy** – Sharing a physical space with another person. This is different than sexual intimacy. My adult son can sit on the couch next to me and play with my hair. I do not let the people at the bus stop do that.

- **Emotional Intimacy** – Sharing what I feel and how my emotions are affected by what I am experiencing.

- **Intellectual Intimacy** – Sharing what I am learning, what I know, what I am thinking, my opinions

- **Spiritual Intimacy** – Sharing what I believe and how I am growing in my relationship with God.

These types of intimacies are the natural result of closeness in a healthy relationship. Casual friendships may have one or two of these intimacies. A good friendship can have four or five. A good marriage has all of these intimacies; faithful sexual intimacy is a special intimacy reserved for marriage.

In Summary

Friends are an important part of a healthy life. We all need good healthy friends. Making friends is a learned skill and well worth putting in the effort. There are many levels of friendships and we need people in each of these levels. Making friends is a learned skill we can improve at any age.

CHAPTER NINE

You have the right to choose when and how your body is touched

One of my fundamental rights is that I get to say when and how my body is touched. People who love me may want a hug and a kiss. Friends and family may put a hand on my arm, touch me in passing, and a hundred other small, loving touches in the normal course of life. I get to choose if I want those touches and I can tell them how I want to be touched or not touched. In a loving family, those guidelines are respected.

Hugs

I like hugs from close family. These touches are part of the pleasant closeness of a safe, nurturing family. There are friends who greet me with a hug, there are friends with whom I never share a hug. This is part of the give and takes of friendship. Preferences about touch are mentioned and respected.

Then there are other people. There was an older gentleman in our church who had read about babies in an orphanage who died for lack of physical contact and hugging. So, he had made it his practice to hug as many people as possible every Sunday morning as a way of providing a kind and welcoming greeting. The problem was that the church hosted a support group for women who had been sexually abused as children and were working to heal from touch violation. Many suffered from Post-Traumatic Stress Disorder, PTSD and most had a revulsion to being touched at some time during their healing process. He wanted to hug everyone to share loving kindness yet could not seem to understand that he should ask permission and accept 'No' for an answer.

Some people are very touch-oriented, and they like to hug a lot. They reach for others all the time. As a professional mental health therapist, I have had these people in my office. As we get up to leave at the end of a counseling session, they reach for me to hug me. Therapeutically, I do not reject them, I just shift so it becomes a side hug. Even though I enjoy being hugged by family and friends, I would rather not be touched by my clients. This is a professional boundary I set. So, in our next session, I will talk with that client about how touch is used in their life, with family and friends, etc. I ask what they are trying to express with the hug. I want them to be able to put that kind, loving expression into words. Then I give them some education about the fact that not all people like to be touched or hugged, mentioning I am one of those. I go on to explain that for people with PTSD, or people who have been violated by unwanted touch, it is an uncomfortable feeling to be touched without permission. I also discuss the difference between:

- Giving a hug –
  - o welcome and with permission.

- Taking a hug –
  - o unwelcome and without permission.

If you really want to share a loving touch, ask permission. Some people who like to be hugged may have a time when it will be painful. If you usually hug your friend every Sunday morning at church and one morning they put a hand up to indicate no, do not get mad or feel rejected. It may have nothing to do with you. Perhaps your friend has a sunburn or back pain, and to hug would be painful that day. But even in the case of 'no' to touch or hug, you could give a "verbal hug" by expressing in words what you wanted to express by touching.

Sometimes adults will tell a child to go hug another person. A child should have the right to say 'no.' When adults force a child into unwanted hugs, they may be setting the child up for future abuse. They are telling the child they have no right to say 'no' to unwanted contact. I encourage parents to train their children that it is ok to politely tell anyone—adult or another child—that they do not wish to be touched.

71

Empowering your child to have a choice means that when they do choose to touch and hug, it is a wonderful, heartfelt action.

If there is a safety or legal issue, the law enforcement people may touch me when I would rather they do not, but that has to do with law or safety. However, here I am discussing all the other times someone wants to touch me.

Equipping Children for Safety

I encourage parents to use clear language for body parts. Clear communication is a good thing. If you teach your child "you have a head, you have an arm, you have a foot you have a hand," and then you whisper, "*you have a down there'*," you have just communicated to you child that they can talk to you about anything that happens to their head, hand, arm, or foot, but that we do not talk about what happens *down there*. When a child abuser is looking for a child to violate, they look for a child who does not talk about important things to parents.

You should use clear medical words for body parts: breasts, vagina, and penis. Using other words can create confusion. One little girl was taught to refer to her private parts as 'cookies.' Then she came home from a friend's birthday party and told Mom that the dog licked her cookies. Mom had to ask a bunch more questions to figure out what actually happened. Another girl was taught to refer to her private parts as peepee. When she was back with Mom after being in the care of her stepdad, she said, "Daddy put his peepee in my peepee." Mom thought sexual abuse had happened, but when it was investigated, the little girl had gone into the bathroom, closed the door, urinated, then left the bathroom without flushing the toilet. Dad then went into the bathroom, shut the door, and urinated, then flushed the toilet that contained both his and her urine.

Sexual Abuse

Abuse is the improper use of something or someone; to use to bad effect or for a bad purpose; to misuse. To treat someone with cruelty or violence, especially doing it again and again. Any action that intentionally harms or injures another person in any way is committing abuse. An abusive situation is where one person is seeking to control the other through abuse.

No one has the right to sexually abuse another person, especially not a child. The laws tell us a child CANNOT give consent for sexual touch. Our laws are designed to protect children.

Non-consensual sexual contact between adults is illegal as well. You get to decide how and when your body is touched and by whom. And you can change your mind. Even if you are naked in bed together and now do not want to be touched, you have the right to say 'No.' A healthy, respectful person who cares about you will honor your 'No.'

In Summary

Your body is yours and you get to decide when and how it is touched. You do not have to put up with unwanted touch. Not unwanted hugs, not unwanted sexual contact. Other people also have the right to choose when they will be touched. If you really want to share a loving touch, ask permission. But even in the case of 'no' to touch or hug, you could give a "verbal hug" by expressing in words what you wanted to express by touching.

CHAPTER TEN

You have the right to treat yourself as well as you treat others

Self or Others?

A common dysfunctional response to abuse or trauma is to pay attention to taking care of others at the expense of your own needs. While there may be short periods when that is appropriate, if you do that long-term your mental, emotional, and physical health can suffer. This dysfunctional habit can greatly hinder your life. Also, it is not necessarily a good thing for other people either. Let's look at some examples.

Oxygen Mask Rule

In every airline flight, the attendants will say some variation of this Oxygen Mask Rule: *"Should the cabin lose pressure, oxygen masks will drop from the overhead area. Please place the mask over your own* mouth *and nose before assisting others."* In the case of the airplane, oxygen masks drop down in situations where the oxygen level has dropped dangerously low. Without the extra oxygen that comes through the mask, people may quickly lose consciousness. If we don't make putting on our own oxygen mask our first priority, we may pass out before we can finish helping someone else get theirs on. The point here is that if you try to help someone else before putting on your own mask, you both may pass out from lack of oxygen. That puts both of you at risk of harm.

Love Others <u>as</u> Yourself

In the Bible, Jesus was asked about the greatest commandment. *"Teacher, which is the greatest commandment in the Law?" Jesus replied: "'Love the Lord your God with all your heart and with all your soul and with all your mind.' This is the first and greatest commandment. And the second is like it: 'Love your neighbor as yourself.' All the Law and the Prophets hang on these two commandments."* Matthew 22:36-40

From this, we find a basis for wanting to treat others well and help them with what they need. Let's unpack this passage. *Love your neighbor as yourself.*

- **Love**—What does it mean to love? We discussed the different concepts of love in chapter one. I believe this means to do what is right; be kind, gentle, merciful; and do what is in the long-term best interests of others.

- **Your neighbor**—Who is your neighbor? Jesus discusses this in Luke 25:37. From that story, it seems to me that our neighbor is anyone we are around and can show kindness and mercy to.

- **As yourself**—What does this mean? It goes back to "love." It is expected that I will care about myself, be kind to myself, show myself gentleness and mercy. And therefore I will also treat others in this way. It does NOT mean that if I treat myself badly I should also treat others badly.

Love Others Instead of Yourself

In my work with people who have experienced trauma, I find people often behave as if Jesus said to love others instead of themselves. Therefore they put everyone else's needs in front of their own. They spend all their time and energy trying to make others happy. Then they feel overwhelmed, exhausted, powerless, and hopeless to make life better. This can lead to burnout, frustration, and anger. It is back to the oxygen mask rule. They are trying to help others put their masks on, but their own strength is fading because they are not giving themselves the basics of what they need in order to stay strong enough to be of help to others. Each person is responsible for their own happiness.

Avoiding Burnout

In order to be able to care for others, we have to care for ourselves. Managing our own self-care includes deliberately planning times in your day to attend to your own needs and maintain your own happiness, physical health, mental health, and spiritual health. If you don't make that a priority, eventually you will not be able to care for others.

What is good self-care? Getting enough rest, eating healthy, adequate exercise, time alone, time with other people, time to be creative, and many other things, large and small, that treat ourselves with love, kindness, and respect. It is about balance. Time to care for self, so that you have the strength to care for others. Setting boundaries helps you to understand what you are responsible for and what is the responsibility of others.

Loving or harmful?

Another principle to look at is to not spend all your time doing for others what they could do for themselves. That could actually be harmful to them. For example, we carry a baby where they need to be because they cannot get there on their own. That is helpful. But if a healthy child is four years old and we are still carrying them around instead of letting them walk, we are harming their ability to strengthen their own muscles and have the freedom of walking and running. That is not helpful. It is also not loving or kind. Setting boundaries of what you will do and won't do can be a loving act.

Setting boundaries; being good to myself and others

A boundary simply defines what is mine and what is not mine; what I am responsible for and what I am not responsible for. How can I set boundaries? First, I am only responsible for that which I have a choice over. Let us look out far then bring it in closer to home. For example, I am not responsible for what the person the next block says to their spouse or the way they choose to do their laundry. That is pretty clear.

Now think about four people who decided to rent a house together. What is each roommate's responsibility for other adults who live in the house? Who is responsible for what they do in the home? Everyone affected by it. If one person dirties all the dishes and never washes any, everyone is affected by that. Some of that might be defined by the rental agreement and in the roommate agreement. Who does each person's laundry? Who cleans each person's bedroom? How are the common areas kept tidy? Who is responsible for the dishes each person dirties?

Boundaries define who is responsible for what. If someone comes in and throws their dirty clothes at you, telling you to wash them, a clear boundary might be, "Whoa, do not put your laundry on me. I am not going to do your laundry; that is your responsibility." They may then accuse me of being selfish, lacking consideration for others, or having a total disregard for anyone else's feelings. That statement is an attempt at manipulation to get what they want. But when they cannot guilt you into doing their laundry, they may finally tell you what the issue really is: "I don't know how to do laundry." Then you can choose to be helpful and talk them through the process, so they learn how to take care of their own needs.

To be unselfish is to be aware of other's needs and the effect of your behavior on others. The golden rule is to treat others like you would like to be treated. We are to love others as we love ourselves. As we talked about earlier in this chapter, that presumes that we love ourselves. We are not to love others instead of ourselves, but as we love ourselves.

Sometimes that means answering "No" to a request. I have my own responsibilities to take care of. If I spend all my time doing what others want, I may not be able to get my own responsibilities done. Sometimes doing what others want is not in their best interest because it may be enabling bad habits or behaviors on their part. For example, the roommate who wants me to do their laundry may not know how to do laundry. If I do it for them, they still do not know how to do laundry. If I say, "No, I will not wash it for you," but I agree to do it with them, teaching them how to do their own laundry for next time, then I am bringing a lifetime benefit to them. If I just do their laundry for them today, that is a single benefit, but not in their best interest. Teaching them how to do laundry benefits them long-term.

In Summary

You have the right to treat yourself as well as you treat others. A common lingering effect of trauma is to have that out of balance, focusing only on the needs of others. When we take good care of ourselves, we then have the capacity to care for others better. It is not helpful to keep doing for others what they can do for themselves. Good boundaries allow us to care for ourselves and care for others in ways that are healthy.

CHAPTER ELEVEN

You have the right not to be responsible for other adult's choices, feelings, and behavior

Each person is responsible for their own choices. Each adult has the opportunity or ability to act independently and make decisions without asking for permission. With that is the duty to deal with or have control over, or be accountable for something within one's power, control, or management. Sometimes people will say, "You made me feel like this or you made me do that," trying to shove the responsibility for their feelings and behaviors onto others. That is not accurate. Let me say again: each person is responsible for their own choices, behaviors, and feelings.

Feelings just happen, informed by our history, our experiences, our beliefs, our thoughts, and our values. We have a choice over our own thoughts, beliefs, values, and behaviors, but what first triggers our feelings may be outside our control. Understand that feelings are in some ways like the weather: something triggers them, and we may not have a lot of control over the fact that the feeling shows up. We do have control over everything that follows. It is like the old saying:

"I cannot keep a bird from flying over my head, but I can keep it from building a nest in my hair."

We may not have much control over a feeling that flashes up, but we do not have to make it welcome, spend time with it and give it a home. We do not have to let it control our behavior, our words, or our choices. Unhealthy responsibility is when I am made to feel responsible for another's choice: "It is your fault I did this." That is the message of a dysfunctional life, not the message of a healthy life. Guilt is an offer; we do not always have to accept other people's offer of guilt. We are not guilty of what others do, only for choices that we make ourselves. That feeling of unease is due to having done something wrong or failed in an obligation that violates a standard of conduct, especially violating the law and involving a penalty. It's worth repeating: we are only guilty of the choices we make ourselves. Unhealthy manipulation happens when people try to shift blame or get others to do what they are responsible for.

We are not responsible for what other adults do even though we are affected by their choices. Some people choose to live in constant drama, like a whirlwind of chaos and problems. When we are around such people, we are buffeted by the winds of their whirlwind, but we do not have to enter their storms.

People with dysfunctional ways of living try to blame you for their feelings and their behavior. We do not have to accept that blame. It does not belong to us and we do not have to take it. One way to handle this is to visualize yourself with a big, clear shield, perhaps similar to the ones that the police use when rioters are throwing things. When someone wants to throw the guilt on you, mentally pull up your shield and let that guilt hit your shield, not your heart. As it slides down the shield away from you, take a look and examine, "Is any of that mine?" If not, then let it slide away from you. If when you look at it there is one small part that is yours, you can take that and deal with it, but let the rest of it drop away.

What we are responsible for

Each one of us is responsible for the choices we make, no matter what we are feeling. Just like you are not responsible for another adult's feelings, they are not responsible for yours.

In most parts of my life, I am a mature adult, a competent professional. But once in a while, maybe when I see pumpkin pie slices, my inner five-year-old can be demanding or want to throw a tantrum to get its own way. "I want the biggest piece of pie!" The feeling may flash up inside me, but I get to choose whether to let it have control of my words or behavior. I can choose to let the calm adult in me simply say to the inner five-year-old, "Now, now, we are going to be polite and share. There is always more pie." The inner five-year-old feelings are not the problem. The problem would be if you let that childlike feeling take over your words and behavior at that moment. There are appropriate times to let the childlike feelings take over. I do not want to hinder my childish emotions entirely, because my inner five-year-old is also the part of me that sees pretty flowers and rejoices in their beauty and takes delight in their colors, giving me feelings of happiness to see the gloriousness of nature and thank God for it.

How to let others know when you are angry, grumpy, or hurting.

It is possible the share what you are feeling without splashing the feelings all over other people. For example, many women have uncomfortable feelings during part of their monthly menstrual cycle. Physical pain and emotional feelings are triggered. That is a fact of life. However, speaking or behaving badly to others is a choice. A person can communicate what they are feeling by simply stating it clearly: "I feel grumpy today" or "I am sad today" or "I feel really mad right now," without making that statement loudly or aggressively. The statements can be made politely, perhaps with a request to not stress them today, since their tolerance level is low.

Heat or light in communicating. When you are angry, are you showing heat or light?

- Anger that is all heat will say hurtful words, such as negative things about people's character, their values, or even their right to breathe air on the planet. Yet they have not said anything about what they feel is wrong or what could be done to improve that. For example, another driver cuts you off in traffic and you yell, *"YOU JERK, WHERE DID YOU LEARN TO DRIVE?"* That is all heat, no light.

- Light is when someone is angry, and they clearly state what the concerns are in neutral language and the results of the problem, and state what they would like done about it and ask for or suggest ways to resolve the concerns. For example: *"It would have helped me if had signaled you were going to pull in front of me so I could have slowed down or stopped."* That is all light, no heat.

Taking the time to be polite and kind in the way we respond to others will help everyone's life go better. Clear communication avoids a lot of hurt feelings and strengthens relationships. When you clearly communicate your feelings, you have a better chance of getting helpful responses. We can ask others to explain more clearly what they mean when they are saying vague or manipulative things. We do not have to be mind-readers.

You do have some responsibility for your child's choices, as well as your response to their feelings. Children are under the control and protection of adults because they are dependents, still learning how to make responsible choices. We provide care and protection for those who are dependent on us, those who cannot care for themselves and rely on someone or something else for aid and support.

I have chosen to be a kind and polite person. It is my choice to not be offensive. But it is not my responsibility if you are offended. I choose to be aware of other people's needs, views, and preferences. Where I can, I am willing to accommodate many of those preferences. But there is a point at which I will choose not to accommodate others. Sometimes someone may be offended by that when they want all the world to go their way. I am not responsible for the fact that they are offended by my refusal to do what they want me to do. It is my responsibility to be kind and polite, but I am not responsible for how they feel.

In summary

I am not responsible for the choices, feelings, or behaviors of other adults. We do not have to accept the unwarranted guilt they may try to put on us. Other people are not responsible for your feelings, choices or behaviors. Each one is responsible for their own. No matter what you are feeling, you always have a choice over your behavior. Polite, clear communication will strengthen relationships.

CHAPTER TWELVE

You have the right to feel angry and leave if you are treated abusively

No matter what we feel, our own behavior is always our own choice. Other people's behavior and words are their own choices too. We do not have to accept bad behavior from others. We can set limits on how we will be treated. It is normal to feel angry if you are treated abusively. That feeling of anger may range in intensity from mild irritation to intense fury and rage.

How do we know what is abuse? Abuse is the improper use of something or someone; to use to bad effect or for a bad purpose; to misuse. To treat someone with cruelty or violence, especially regularly or repeatedly. Any action that intentionally harms or injures another person in any way is committing abuse and is illegal. When a truly abusive situations exist because one party is seeking to control the other through force, coercion or manipulation.

These are some of the recognized types of abuse:

- **Physical injury**, including an injury that is inflicted by non-accidental means that results in harm.
- **Neglect,** including failure through action or omission to provide and maintain food, shelter, medicine, supervision, protection, or nurturance to such a degree that a child's, or vulnerable adult's, health and safety are endangered.
- **Mental abuse**, which is a continuing pattern of rejecting, terrorizing, ignoring, isolating, or corrupting, resulting in serious mental and emotional damage.
- **Threat of harm** is threatening or subjecting someone to severe harm via physical abuse, sexual abuse, mental injury, or other abuse or neglect.
- **Sexual abuse**, which is nonconsensual sexual contact between adults or any sexual contact in which a child or teen younger than 18 years is used to sexually stimulate another person.
- **Financial abuse** includes having money or other property stolen, being defrauded, being put under pressure in relation to money or other property, and having money or other property misused.
- **Emotional abuse** includes intimidation, verbal aggression, manipulation, and

humiliation that, as a pattern of behavior, diminishes another person's sense of self-worth, identity, and dignity. This often results in depression, anxiety, suicidal thoughts or behaviors, and perhaps post-traumatic stress disorder (PTSD).

- **Spiritual abuse** is when religious authority figures use the power of their position to shame, coerce, or control others.

No one has the right to abuse another person. Everyone has a choice over their own behavior. Behavior is the way in which one acts or conducts oneself, especially toward others, sometimes affected by external reactions to one's environment. Feeling angry, hurt, or afraid is okay. Any feelings are okay, but remember behavior is always a choice and abusive behavior is NEVER okay.

If you need to leave an abusive situation, there are people who will help you. You can set up a safety plan and find support people you can call to help you leave.

For a free list of resources is available at:

www.FaithfulHabits.com/ Fundamentals

Why victims find it hard to leave.

Often people wonder why it is so hard for a victim to leave an abusive relationship. There are a number of reasons.

- **Familiar Experience** - They may have grown up in an abusive home and so they see this as the ordinary, unchangeable way of life. They do not expect anything different so it does not occur to them that they can leave.

- **Isolation** -Abusers work to isolate the victim so the victim feels like they have no resources and no support even if they wanted to leave. Victims can feel like no one cares about them, that they are alone in this situation.

- **Low Self-esteem** - Overtime in subtle or blatant ways, abusers work to erode the victim's self-esteem, telling them they are worthless. No one else would want them. They are lucky that the abuser even wants them a little bit. The victim begins to believe the abuser and believes they have no way out.

- **Learned Helplessness** - Over time, victims can be taught that they are helpless, that they would not survive without the abuser. And the victim can over time come to believe that lie.

- **Valid Fear** - Victims realize this is abuse and they want to get out, but they are afraid the abuser will hunt them down and kill them or their families. This happens, so the fear is valid.

- **Love for Children** - When children are part of the household, the victim may not see a way to leave and still have their children with them, so they stay in order to be around their children and protect them as much as they can.

- **Hope for Change** - Often the victim has hope that the abuser will change, and things will get better. Abusers often promise it will not happen again. That might be possible, but leaving is the best option in many cases.

Every situation is different and there are many other reasons it is hard for victims to leave. Helping victims of abuse is about helping them overcome the barriers to leaving an abusive situation and moving toward healing and health.

Domestic violence and abuse have some recognizable common cycles. Starts out everything is okay. Then a tension starts to build. A feeling of dread hangs over each day. The feeling can be like walking on eggshells just waiting for the explosion. Then the explosion happens: abuse happens. Then the abuser may blame the victim, or the abuser may apologize and say it will never happen again, expressing how sorry they are. At this point, a pleasant period starts. The abuser is trying to be kind, generous, and helpful. Then the pleasant period begins to fade to a more ordinary period where everything is okay. This is where the cycle started and where it returns to.

The cycle of abuse gets repeated over and over. What changes is the intensity. Often the abuse becomes more intense, more frequent. The period of living on eggshells becomes the biggest part of the cycle. Without intervention, this cycle can become so intense that there are broken bones, or someone may even die.

No one has the right to harm another person. When the abuse victim strikes out in violence, they may be trying to defend themselves in the only way they know-how, but meeting evil with evil means evil wins. If you are abusive back to an abuser, you are becoming like them, and you are letting evil win. A better option is to leave the situation. Escaping may be hard and dangerous, but it's often the right choice.

Once you leave, you can find healing for yourself. As you grow and heal, learn to value yourself, and set healthy boundaries, you are in a better position to assess if you want to risk reconnecting with someone who has abused you in the past. Have they gone through a learning, healing, and growing process of their own? Or are they still in that same place they were? Change is possible, but you can only change yourself. You cannot make an abuser change. That choice is up to them.

The dance of change

When you decide to make a change, you will affect those close to you. Relationships can be like a dance. Both of you know the steps and how the dance usually goes. Each time one person moves, the other person has to move to stay in step. When one of you decides to make a change, when one of you decides to heal and grow healthy, it will affect the other. The first response the other makes is to try to pull you back into the same dance, to get you back into step with the dance they know. If you will not be pulled back into that unhealthy dance, they have a choice to make. They either have to pull away and leave the dance, or they have to change to learn how to stay in step with you in this new dance. It is their choice.

In summary

You have a right to feel angry if you are treated abusively. You do not have to stay in an abusive situation. There are resources to help you to leave an abusive situation and be safe. There are many types of abuse, but they all exist because one party is seeking to control the other through force, coercion or manipulation. Victims of abuse often find it hard to leave. There are resources available to help. You have the right to be safe.

PART THREE

FREEDOM FUNDAMENTALS

Freedom rights are the freedoms that we have individually and collectively to make our own choices of what we want to do and how we want to move forward in our life. These include the responsibilities and duties we have as adults.

- You have the right to your own privacy, personal space, and time.
- You have the right to make your own decisions about your life.
- You have the right to ask questions about anything that affects your life.
- You have the right to request what you want.
- You have the right to earn and control your own resources.
- You have the right to not be liked by everyone.

This part of the book will expand on each of the freedom rights above, exploring how we live out these rights, to help you to understand your rights as a human being. Also providing a road map of how you can respect these rights for yourself and respect these rights for others.

CHAPTER THIRTEEN

You have the right to your own privacy, personal space, and time

We have a right to privacy. To have privacy is to be free from being observed or disturbed by other people, to be let alone. Privacy allows us to ponder our own thoughts, observe our own feelings, and make decisions. Places we expect physical privacy are in bathrooms, bedrooms, and our living spaces, but there are levels of privacy. We let family and friends into places in our lives that we do not let strangers.

Introverts tend to need more privacy than extroverts do. There's nothing wrong with that. Introverts enjoy time alone or with one or two other people they care about. They like time to ponder life deeply and think through the implications and contexts of life. Then, when they are ready, they are willing to be with others and to share.

Some types of privacy

- Privacy of our own bodies
- Privacy of thought and feelings
- Privacy of who we hang out with
- Private behavior and actions
- Privacy of personal communication

Modified Privacy

There are times in our lives when we choose to accept a modified level of privacy. For example:

- When people get married, they share their lives and gladly give up a lot of individual privacy.
- In the safe confidential space of therapy, people give up privacy in the hope of finding healing and growth.
- When we go camping, we may be sharing living space.
- People who choose to be roommates in a community living situation give up some of their privacy.
- In a recovery community, some privacy is given up in order to keep the community safer and to help facilitate the healing and growing process.
- In a rental, landlords have the right to enter for allowed purposes and with appropriate notice.
- A homeowner must allow the tax accessor to enter, with notice. If there is a health department concern, the county health depart

may enter, with notice. If police have probable cause, they may enter.

- Individual privacy is briefly given up for drug testing in order to keep a workplace or recovery community safer for everyone.

One of the ways we show integrity and respect is how we treat others' rights to privacy. Respecting others' privacy is not just when someone is watching or may know what you are doing. Someone with integrity, who respects other people's privacy, would not read another person's diary even if it were left open in a common area.

In order to be in relationships, we work out a privacy level that each person is comfortable with. The respectful, shared privacy of a marriage allows the trust between partners to grow deeply when intimacy is shared, and very little privacy is needed between them. Parents teach children about acceptable privacy levels in their home and out in the world.

Different families and different living situations, like roommates, community living, and different cultures, have different standards of privacy. Some families knock on bedroom doors, waiting for a response before entering. In other families, parents have established the right to walk into a child's room. Expectations of privacy in a living situation is a good topic to discuss amongst the people living together so that everyone can express their preferences and the expectations can be developed together.

When there is abuse in a home, privacy tends to be one-sided. The abuser wants privacy but denies it to everyone else. Part of abuse is to deny privacy of thought, opinion, space, body, and resources. An abused child who grows up being taught they do not have a right to privacy may unknowingly violate the privacy of others. However, this does not give adults excuses for violating privacy, because anyone can learn where privacy boundaries are in life. What we experienced as a small child is not our fault, but we are responsible for the kind of adult we become.

In a recovery community, individuals have chosen to give up privacy in order to enjoy the benefits of the community. In order to enjoy the advantages of the recovery community, the individuals accept some limits to their privacy. These limits may include sharing living space, sleeping in a room with others, eating in shared dining spaces. They choose to accept a modified level of privacy because the benefits they receive are more important to them at this time than maintaining privacy.

In Summary

You have a right to privacy. Privacy of your own body. Privacy of thought and feelings. Privacy of who we hang out with. Private behavior and actions. Privacy of personal communication. There are times and situations where modified privacy is appropriate.

CHAPTER FOURTEEN

You have the right to make your own decisions about your life

You are in control of your choices, of how you make a decision when faced with two or more possibilities. Making good choices can include judging the merits of multiple options. We make choices based on our values and on the templates developed while making past choices. Part of a healthy life is intentionally choosing your values and intentionally developing the decision-making templates that will be in line with your values and your goals.

You have the right to make your own choices, and live with the consequences of those choices, whether they are good, bad, or neutral. We all make hundreds of choices every day. When to get up, what attitude to face the day with, what to wear, where to go, what to do.

Many of these choices are almost automatic because they are informed by the choices we made long ago and the habits we have developed. Many choices are informed by more recent choices. For example, the choice of what to wear today may be informed by the choice of what clothes you have when you last did laundry and where your clothes are. The choice of what to do today may be informed by your choice of occupation. If you choose to enter a community living situation, today's choices will be directed by that earlier choice. Every day you have the choice of your attitude of how you will face the day.

We are responsible for anything we have a choice over. We are not responsible for what we do not have a choice over. For example, when it is raining, we are not responsible for the rain. However, we are responsible to dress appropriately for the rain and to have gathered resources to be able to dress appropriately for the rain. We are responsible for our own attitude about the rain. Therefore, even though the rain isn't in our control, whether the rainy day is a good day, a bad day, or a neutral day is generally under our control.

Life has problems. Stress happens to everyone. But misery is optional. When problems happen, the day may get hard. However, it is not the day's problems that make misery; it is the way we face the problems that can create misery for ourselves and others. Our choice of attitude about problems will make the stress even harder or will avoid adding to troubles.

How we get our values

In chapter four we explored the fact that you get to choose your own values. But when we were children, we were handed a set of values by the important adults in our lives. Some of these values may have been directly taught. You probably were told things like, "We do not do those things; we do these things." That is an expression of the values of your people. Other values we picked up on our own as we understood how our world worked and we saw how people interacted. Other values we were taught in school. Entertainment media showed us examples of people's values. Trauma, bullying, abuse, and stress affect how we understand the values of the world and our own place in it. Before we were teenagers, we had already accepted a lot of values that informed our behavior and gave us templates for decision-making. As adults, we get to examine our values and the way we make decisions and make intentional choices about what is important to us and why.

At some points in our lives, we begin to decide intentionally what kind of person we wanted to be. We would think, "Those were my parent's values, teachers' values, the values of the society around me, but what do I choose as my own values?" This is not a one-time event; it happens a number of times in big and small ways throughout our lives. What kind of person do you want to be? It is a choice we get to make each day. The values we hold are what informs the way we make decisions.

Some common values people respect

- **Dignity** is the inherent value and worth everyone is born with. Dignity is the value and importance a person has that leads to respect for themselves and others.
- **Faithfulness** means to be firm in adherence to promises or in observance of duty; steadfast in affection or allegiance, true to the facts, to a standard, or to an original.
- **Forgiveness** is about extending mercy to those who have harmed you, even if they do not deserve to be forgiven. There are two directions of forgiveness: giving forgiveness and receiving forgiveness. Choosing to give forgiveness is an active process, which includes a decision to let go of any negative feelings or thoughts of getting back at a person for the wrong they have done to you. Receiving forgiveness means you have agreed with the other individual that you have done wrong and therefore you need forgiveness. God chooses to offer forgiveness to all who come to him, confessing their wrongs, and asking for forgiveness.
- **Friendship** is a relationship with a person you know, and who knows you, a mutual bond of like and trust. Different levels of friendship include casual friends, good friends, and the friends with which you have a close and deep bond, A close friend has your long-term best interest at heart.
- **Kindness** is to show consideration toward others, to be aware of their needs, to have a

good nature or disposition, to be helpful and caring about other people.

- **Loyalty** is trusting someone to have your long-term best interest at heart. Someone who is faithful to one's oath, commitments, or obligations.
- **Peacefulness** is a state of being sound and complete. Having harmony and wholeness. The absence of strife or war. To make amends and put things right.
- **Respect** is a way of treating or thinking about something or someone; polite behavior, treating people in a positive manner that acknowledges them for who they are and/or what they are doing. Due regard for the feelings, wishes, rights, or traditions of others.
- **Responsibility** is having a duty to deal with or have control over. Being the person who is answerable or accountable for something within your control, power, or management. The ability or opportunity to make decisions without authorization and to act independently.
- **Safety** is the condition of being protected from potential harm or being unlikely to cause danger, risk, or injury.

You get to make choices about who your friends are and how much of your life and thoughts you share with them. The choices you make about your friends can affect your behaviors and values. It has been said that you will become like the five people you spend the most time with. Look around, is that who you want to become? Your friends can take you closer to your values or farther away from them. They can support you as you move toward your goals or they can hinder your progress. Your choice of friends and your choice of how much to be influenced by them has consequences in your life, for better or worse. If you choose values and then choose friends who share those values the consequences will be that you have support as you move toward your life goals. If you walk with wise companions, you will become wiser; if you choose to be with bad companions, you will suffer harm. Your choice, your consequences.

Your choice of where you live can have consequences on your options for work. If you choose to live in the country, there may not be access to public transportation. So, the consequence of living in the country may be that you have to provide your own transportation to a workplace or that you only have work options that are nearby. If you choose to live in the city, the consequences may be easy access to public transportation and a wide variety of jobs to choose from. However, the country may have healthier air to breathe and a calmer lifestyle. Living in the city may provide more access to health care and a greater variety of options for leisure activities. There is no right or wrong choice. Each choice has benefits and challenges. When you are making a choice, it is good to look at the costs and benefits of each option you have so you can make the best available choice for you. I mention "available choice" because there may be ten choices but perhaps five of those will not work at all due to something like finances or health considerations that you cannot change.

Even in a more controlled environment, like a community living situation, you have lots of choices. You chose to enter the situation, or you chose the behavior that ended in that situation. But you still have choices within the situation. You get to choose whether to obey the community guidelines or to work against them. You get to choose the attitude with which you face each day. If you voluntarily entered the situation, you could voluntarily leave it. But you may choose to stay because of the benefits that you have while living in the community. You alone are responsible for the choices you make.

While your choices are your responsibility alone, they can have positive or negative consequences for other people, just like you are affected, for good or ill, by the choices of others. Perhaps you have wondered, where is God when other people's choices hurt me? It is my understanding that God gave us free will, and with that free will we can choose to do right and love God, bring value to the world, and help others live to be better, or we can use our free will to hurt ourselves and others, to break and destroy and damage our own world and the world around us, making life more difficult for others.

When someone chooses to drink alcohol to the point of being impaired and then they decide to drive a motor vehicle, they are choosing to put at risk not only their own safety but the safety of others around them. Their choice to drink and drive may kill or

115

cripple an innocent bystander. Why would God allow that? In my understanding of God and his relationship to his creation, us, our free-will choice to love God and to do right is so valuable that God lets us make our own choices. He will not demand that we love him. Instead, he gives us the opportunity to choose to love him or not, to obey him or not. Giving us that free will means there will be a lot of wrong choices made, and because our actions always affect more than ourselves, these choices can hurt both self and others. But God is able to redeem those wounds and walk with the ones who have been hurt, making something good come out of that wrong.

In my life, I was hurt as a child by the free-will choices of the adults in my life. God not only comforted me in the midst of that pain, but he also healed the wounds in my life and used the compassion and insight I received through those experiences to lead me to become a professional counselor to help others heal from the wounds of life. The benefit I received later is much more valuable than the losses I endured as a child.

We always have choices in life—we just may not like the choices we have. Some choices seem harder than others. Sometimes no option available is to our liking. Life is like that at times. When you do not like the path you have chosen, you get to change your mind and make a different choice. Choose for yourself this day whom you will serve.

In Summary

It is your life, and you have the right to make your own decisions about your attitude, how you will use your resources, and the values you choose to hold as important to you. These decisions added together over months and years bring your life more in line with your values or put you in conflict with your values, perhaps leading you to neglect what you hold most important. You are responsible for your choices.

CHAPTER FIFTEEN

You have the right to ask questions about anything that affects your life

We have the right to ask questions about all the things that affect our lives. We need the important, necessary, and supporting information when we have decisions to make, so we can make the best-informed decisions. When something has changed and it affects our lives, we may need to ask for additional information, so we know what our best response is to the change. It is normal that we ask questions when we are seeking to learn and grow; we need lots of information so we can understand more about the world around us.

Being curious is a healthy part of life. Curiosity is an important habit. It lets your mind be active, not passive. Your mind wants to understand things and actively figure things out. When we are curious, we have a strong desire to know or learn something. We ask questions and search for patterns and answers. Curiosity opens up new worlds and possibilities. The world is full of wonders, small and big. By being curious, you bring excitement into your life about what you will discover. There are always new things that attract your attention; there are always new thoughts to think and new questions to ask.

We see the right to ask questions lived out in the normal question-asking behavior of young children. The world is new to them, so there is much they want to know. They have an unlimited supply of questions. When the adults around them are kind and answer their questions patiently and even encourage their questions, their knowledge and understanding grows by leaps and bounds. Question-asking is vital to a child's development.

Parents can grow tired of constantly answering questions, particularly when the questions are about why the child has to do something they were just asked to do. Parents may reply tersely, "Because I said so!" That is not a helpful response to a curious child. It is better to calmly tell the child, "Do what I told you to do now, then later, when we have more time, we can discuss the why." At a later time the parent can explain. When the parent doesn't know the answer to what is being asked, it is perfectly okay to answer, "I don't know." Perhaps it is a teaching moment where parent and child can try to find the answer together. Sometimes children will ask questions it is not appropriate to give them the answer to at that time or at their young age. Adults can be straightforward and reply, "That is not a question I will answer for you right now."

While being curious and asking questions is often a good thing, we do not always have a right to know everything we may want to know. Some information is private and only available to those who need to know. When we are about to ask questions, it is good to stop and take a moment to figure out if this is a "need to know," a "right to know," or a "want to know" kind of question. What do we want to know? Often, everything about everything. But do we have the right to know this information? Do we need the information? How does it affect our life? At times we may want information that we have no right to; it is the confidential information of others. Sometimes we want to know information so we can figure out how to manipulate things to our own advantage. Many times, what we want to know is just that—a want— and we have no right to or need for the information. We may have the desire or craving to know, maybe because we are nosy and want to gossip to others about it. That is not a good reason to be asking. That information is not necessary to help you and it could be damaging to others. Others have a right to refuse your request for information you have no right to.

A person who likes to gossip wants to know everything about everybody. They engage in casual conversations that reveal other people's personal information and may tell things that are not confirmed or potentially even untrue. In a healthy, functional life, we respect other people's privacy and

121

train ourselves to be okay with not knowing about everything or everyone. Therefore, we only ask for what we need to know. Respecting people's privacy means we do not gossip about other people or ask for information we have no right to know.

Before you ask questions, figure out what you really want to know and why. Is there a valid reason you need to know this information? Does it affect your life and choices? If you do need information, try to figure out exactly what you need to know. Can you clearly word your request? Make it easy to understand or interpret. Be transparent about what you need the information for and why.

Sometimes people ask the wrong question. They may ask a driver who just parked a vehicle, "What made you think you could park there?" when the underlying question is, "When are you going to get out of my way so I can use that area again?" Even if you get the answer to the first question, you still will not know the answer to your underlying question. Also, think about the needs of the other person in this situation.

We have the right to ask questions of others. Others have the right to ask questions of us. We have the responsibility to answer questions with integrity. When I am asked a question I do not want to answer, I do not have to lie or deceive. With integrity, I can simply say "That is information I choose not to share." And if they ask, "Why not?" I simply reply, "That is also information I choose not to share." I am modeling that not all questions have to be answered while showing it is still okay to ask. Learning to have more integrity helps you to have a reputation for being dependable and for only asking for what you need.

Integrity has three meanings.

- To have integrity is to be true and honest, someone we can depend on.
- To have integrity is to be integrated. What we are on the inside, we are on the outside. What we are like with our friends, we are at the workplace. What we are on Friday night, we are on Sunday morning. Everything about us, our values, and the way we treat people is integrated into every part of our life.
- To have integrity means to be whole and complete and fit for a purpose. For example, we would say that a water bottle has integrity if it does not leak. It is whole and complete and fit for its purpose.

To grow in integrity is to grow in all three of these areas. When you have integrity, people can rely on you. You are consistently responsible, only asking for what you need. Therefore, they are a lot more willing to listen to your requests and consider them positively.

Destructive effects happen to trust and relationships when we sneak, hide, deceive, or steal. If we are told no and we sneak around, figuring out how to get what we want anyway, we damage our ability to ask questions and get positive answers in the future because we have broken trust. Sometimes people will say, "I did not lie" while they argue about the exact words that were spoken and try to justify what they did. But it is not about the exact words used; it is about the intent to deceive. They misrepresent the truth for the purpose of causing someone to accept a distortion as true.

If I tell you that my son had his birthday dinner in the state dining room of the White House, every word of that is true. But if I do not mention that it was his 2nd birthday, he was in a stroller, we were on a public tour of the White House, he got fussy, and I gave him his bottle and a few bites of cereal to quiet him down while we happened to be in the state dining room, I have given a totally different impression of the event. If I tell you I was traveling over a hundred miles an hour along the freeway, every word is true, but if I do not mention I was a passenger in a small airplane at 500 feet altitude, you really do not have the truth. That is a different picture than the one you built up in your mind.

Question or Request

To ask questions or to make requests are similar and overlap in a lot of ways, but the two concepts have different intentions. The difference between a request and a question is that to ask a question is usually to enquire, to seek information, while a request is to express a need or a desire for something you want. In chapter 16, we will explore your right to ask for what you want.

In Summary

You have the right to ask questions about anything that affects your life. Asking questions is a normal, healthy behavior. We do not always have a right to know everything we may want to know. Some information is private and only available to those who need to know. When we are about to ask questions, it is good to stop and take a moment to figure out if this is a "need to know," a "right to know," or a "want to know" kind of question. Others have the right to ask questions of us. We have the responsibility to answer questions with integrity.

CHAPTER SIXTEEN

You have the right to request what you want

No person is an island. We all need other people: their support and what they can bring to us and do for us. Likewise, other people need us: our support and what we can bring to them. We bring benefit to other people. Requesting what we need is a normal part of the give and take of healthy life. Others fulfill our needs, and we fulfill the needs of others. It is the way the world works. Learning how and when to request what you want is the focus of this chapter.

What do you really want?

A good place to start is to know what you really want. For example, if you are asking your child, "Turn off that noisy game," is that really what you want? Do you want your child to not be playing that game because you want them to be doing something else?

Or do you want the game not to be played? Or do you want peace and quiet because of what you are doing? If what you want is peace and quiet, turning off that game may not get you what you need. Your child may just go to a different and possibly noisier activity. You get frustrated with your child, and your child does not understand why. The game is off, but you still do not have what you need because you did not ask for it. If instead, you would have asked "Could you play quieter, please?" your child has a better chance of understanding what you really want and giving you that. When we ask for what we really want, we have a much better chance of getting it.

Making clear requests helps our relationships to have less stress. As a therapist, I often work with couples and families who have communication struggles simply because they are not asking for what they want or believing what each other says. They are expecting each other to be mind-readers and understand the implication of what is wanted without having to directly ask for it. That creates hurt feelings and unnecessary stress within the family. Clear communication of needs is a part of letting your yes be yes and your no be no. Make clear requests for what you need and believe the words others say. That can help them learn to make clear requests as well.

Why do you need it?

When asking for what you really want, in order to obtain an answer, response, information, or action, form the request in a way that makes sense to the person you are asking. The temptation is to ask only using points to tell why you really want and need this. Those are valid points but do not forget to add in the reasons why it is good for others for you to get a positive response.

For example, if you are asking to have your work equipment upgraded, it not just because your life will be made easier at work, but also because you will be able to be more productive for the company, the quality of your work will go up, or whatever else is true in your case. When you show your boss how your request will also bring benefit to others and the goal of the company, you have a better chance of a positive response.

The other person's needs

When thinking about how to ask your questions, it is good to also look at the concern from the other person's point of view. What do they need? What could be their possible reasons for doing what they are doing? Then think about why it is in their best interest to give you what you ask for.

When and how we make requests matters

You have a better chance of getting the answer you want when you are respectful and considerate of other people. It's also important to ask at the right time. If you make a request when someone is super busy and stressed, their quickest way to deal with you is a curt 'No'. But, if you asked the same question when the person is not stressed and when they have a free moment, they may have time to consider your question and you are more likely to get a positive response.

Every Boss Has a Boss

When you make a request to your boss in order to obtain an answer, response, information, or action, remember they likely have a boss over them as well. We easily see this with middle managers of big companies. There are bosses of bosses and boards of directors and shareholders. All these have needs and all the bosses may have to justify why they said yes to your request to the person above them. Help them out by giving them the information they need. This is not only true in large corporations, though. Even small companies have bosses above their boss. A sole-owner business has to please customers. Customers are a type of boss. If they do not like the product at that quality, type, or price, they may buy from a different business. When you keep in mind what other people may need as well and provide reasons why this will be good for all concerned, you have a much better chance of a positive response.

Accepting no for an answer

Sometimes you know why you need something, and you ask clearly and politely and at an appropriate time, and the answer is still 'No'. Life is filled with No. Part of being a healthy adult is learning to accept no graciously. That will leave the door open for you to possibly ask again in another way at another time. The person may be more willing to listen to your requests in the future because you stayed polite and respectful in accepting their no this time. If you got mad and argued loudly and strongly, the other person is more likely to make that a firm and permanent 'No,' and not even be willing to discuss it with you again, ever.

When you get a 'No' to your request, accept it graciously. Then see if you can find out the reasons. Perhaps the objection is something you did not think to explain, and a simple additional explanation may turn a no into a yes. Or perhaps the reason is something you never considered, and you need to go back and think again about how to meet their need and your need too. Look for a win/win solution. Be patient and take time to reformulate the request, gearing it toward the self-interest of the person you are asking. Waiting patiently and presenting the request in this new way later can work to your benefit. Include information that will help them in explaining to their boss why they granted your request.

Requests to governmental authorities

Making a request of governmental authority is a little different. There are thousands of pages of governmental guidelines on how requests are to be made and the criteria for approving or denying the requests. You can spend all your energy railing against the government and getting mad at the front-line employees, but none of that will get your request approved. Most of the people we deal with in the government do not have the power to go outside of the guidelines. You are just making their day harder and frustrating yourself when you take out your frustration on them. I suggest you try a way more likely to get valid requests approved.

Ways to make it more likely to get a helpful response:

- First, adjust your attitude. Be grateful. Recognize the authority is instituted by the government and by God and their main purpose is to do you good.
- Be kind to the people who work for the government. They deal with the public all day long and many of the public are frustrated and rude. Be a standout: be polite, civil, patient, and kind in all of your dealings with them.
- Do your homework, read up and find out what is required for the topic you want to be approved.
- Be patient if you find out you may have missed a step. Humbly ask what you need to do to move forward.
- Be patient. There is always more work to do than the time allotted in government work. That is because citizens do not want to pay any more taxes than we have to. That affects how many government workers there are.
- This is not the time to rail against wastes in government or your latest political views and frustrations. You have other means to address those issues through voting and advocacy. Stay focused on this one task at hand.

- If you have done everything and the answer is still 'no', ask about your next step. In most cases, there is an appeal process where you can ask to have the decision reconsidered.
- Be patient and endure. Many applications take two or three appeals to get a final positive resolution.

No was the best answer

Sometimes no matter what we do, the final answer is still no. If you have exhausted all your avenues of appeal, perhaps it is time to just accept this answer is no. Perhaps God has a different path in mind for you. Prayerfully ask and look for it.

In the 1990s, my life got really stressful. Things were in an upheaval not of my own making. It was chaos, and my life was pushed out of the way I knew and onto ways I found scary and different. I was upset and desperately wanted God to "fix this." I prayed earnestly for that repair, meaning, I wanted him to put my life back together the way I was used to. God's answer to me seemed to be a solid No. Instead, he set me on a path to healing my emotional wounds from a traumatic childhood that greatly hindered my adult life. He led my life in a different direction with a lot of new, healthy options I had never thought of. If God had answered my prayer to put my life back the way I was familiar with, I would still be living on poverty's edge; dealing with Post-Traumatic Stress Disorder, anxiety, and panic attacks; isolated; and alone. Instead, 20 years later, I have a master's degree in counseling. I have fulfilling work I love, helping wounded people heal and grow. I have a lot of friends and a rich social life, and I finally was able to buy a house. No was the best answer to my prayer at that time, because though that No God moved me into a happier, more fulfilling life. I was blessed by that No.

In summary:

Requesting what we need is a normal part of the give and take of healthy life. Think through the actual things you need and ask at the right time and place. Make clear, polite requests, thinking about how your request will affect others. Accept a no graciously and think about if you can appeal the decision at another time with more information. Or accept a final no and go on to seek what else you can do.

CHAPTER SEVENTEEN

You have the right to earn and control your own resources

Your resources are anything that helps you achieve what you want to do, such as money, materials, support, supply, skills, knowledge, energy, or education, anything that gives you the ability to deal with life and problems effectively. You get to decide how your resources are used. We all have many more resources available to us than we will ever use. There are public resources provided by our government, there are resources proved by organizations and the resources we have direct control over. We also have the ability to pray, asking God to help us. Many of our resources we take for granted. For example, our ability to think, plan assess the different options in life and make choices of how we will live.

Since you can make choices about your resources, you are the responsible person in control of what happens to your resources. Are you careful to treat your things with respect, to maintain them well, to use them like they are supposed to be used? If you damage your resources, do you expect others to replace them for you? That is like a child deliberately breaking a toy and throwing a tantrum expecting the adults to replace it. The natural consequence of wasting or damaging your resource is that the resource is no longer available for you. Taking good care of your resources helps you to have a better life. The Bible has a lot to say about being diligent, caring for your resources, and working to provide for your needs.

For you, yourselves know how you ought to follow our example. We were not idle when we were with you, nor did we eat anyone's food without paying for it. On the contrary, we worked night and day, laboring and toiling so that we would not be a burden to any of you. We did this, not because we do not have the right to such help, but in order to offer ourselves as a model for you to imitate. For even when we were with you, we gave you this rule: "The one who is unwilling to work shall not eat." We hear that some among you are idle and disruptive. They are not busy; they are busy bodies. Such people, we command and urge in the Lord Jesus Christ to settle down and earn the food they eat.
2 Thessalonians 3:7-12

We make a lot of choices every day, we are faced with judging the merits of multiple possibilities. We have the right to make our own choices about how our resources are used, and that includes the responsibility to use them appropriately. What we have control over we are also accountable for how we handle. The freedom to act independently and make decisions without asking others for permission comes with the responsibility to act wisely. If you choose to spend your month's income on games and pleasure, should you expect someone else to pay for your housing and food? You alone are responsible for the choices you make.

How we use our resources demonstrates what our values really are. If we say that we care about others, and yet behave in self-centered ways that make life harder for others; which one is our most important value? Behavioral values are the values demonstrated by the things we do and the choices we make. How we use resources demonstrates what we feel is important to us. You get to choose your values and whether or not to live in line with your values.

Scarcity mentality, abundance mentality

A greedy person has a scarcity mentality. They behave as if there is a very limited supply of resources and if someone else gets any it means they will be without. They see all other people as competition for scarce resources. They are always grasping for more and hold things tightly when they have them. For example, they may not want their family and friends to have any other friends, as if they are afraid there is not enough friendship to go around, and they must guard what little there is. As a result, their friends and family may feel smothered and pull away. A clingy, greedy person may end up with very few friends. A kind and generous person generally has lots of friends. They encourage their family and friends to become friends with one another and make other friends because they have an abundance mentality, knowing that there is a lot of friendship available in the world and shared friends can mean lots more fun and good times. A greedy person doe does not volunteer because "you don't get paid for that." A generous person volunteers often, knowing they get paid richly in satisfaction, not money.

Generosity is its own reward. There is a delight in giving to others, seeing them have more resources. When we are generous with our time, life is better for everyone. There is a joyful satisfaction in being able to do for others what they may not be able to do for themselves. It also builds a sense of contentment because the generous person realizes just how blessed they are. Generosity begins at home. Are you taking care of yourself and those who are dependent on you, so others are not burdened? And from there you can together be generous with others.

How much is enough?

John D Rockefeller was the richest man on the planet in the 19th century. A reporter once asked him, "How much money is enough?" Rockefeller answered with a smile, "Just a little bit more."

Where do all our resources come from? We could say, "I work hard for every dime I have; nobody gave me anything." Yet who gave you the ability to work? So many of our resources come directly from God and from other people. When you worked hard, are you employed? Then someone gave you a job. Are you self-employed? Then customers are buying your products and services. In all our resources, we are connected to other people. When it comes to what's in our house, we would not have these things unless someone made them, or we learned how to make them. Even then, they are made from materials provided by someone else or out of natural materials in creation provided by God.

> *For who makes you different from anyone else?*
> *What do you have that you did not receive?*
> *And if you did receive it, why do you*
> *boast as though you did not?*
> *1 Corinthians 4:7*

I drive a car that is more than 10 years old. There are some irritations with it. The driver's window no longer rolls down. The turn signal will no longer turn itself off. It has a few scratches and dents. Once in a while, when I see a new car drive by, I may feel like I am deprived. There is a new car, and I am driving this old thing with all its issues. But then I look out my window and I see people waiting at the bus stop in the rain and I am grateful. I am warm and dry inside a car that lets me drive where I want to, when I want to. Whether I am frustrated with a scarcity mentality or blessed with an abundance mentality is

141

a choice I get to make. I am grateful for my old car. By the way, my old car has a feature on it I cannot get on a new car. It is paid for!

In Summary

We all have access to lots of resources. You have the right to earn and control your own resources. You get to decide how your resources are used. You are the responsible person for what happens to your resources. You get to decide if you will have a scarcity mentality, poverty mentality, or abundance mentality. You get to decide whether you will live in the generosity of an abundance mentality or in the struggle of a scarcity mentality. Contentment is not the fulfillment of what I want, but the realization of how much I already have.

CHAPTER EIGHTEEN

You have the right to not be liked by everyone

Popular people

Some people seem to be naturally popular, while others are not as popular. However, no one is universally liked by everyone. That is okay. We do not have to be liked by everyone, but when the person who does not like us is in our family, or extended family, or in our workplace, which can make life harder than it needs to be. You can try every way you know how to make them like you, and nothing seems to work. How can you deal with that?

If it is possible,
as far as it depends on you,
live at peace with everyone.
Romans 12:18

The key phrase here is "as far as it depends on you." That statement to be at peace is tempered by what is under our own control. Let us look closer at that. What are the things that depend on me? The basics of self-inventory are good to do to see if there is a valid reason that someone may not like you or want to be around you. There is a lot that is under our control:

- Reputation. Who are you? What are your characteristics? What would you like your reputation to be? You get to choose.
- Behavior. How do you treat people? Are you kind? Polite?
- Demeanor. Are you arrogant or humble? Patient or rude?
- Personal care. Do you smell bad? Do you look unkempt or uncared for?
- Social habits. Do you talk too much? Are you a loud talker or a high talker? Do you talk too little or too quietly? Do you lurk in social situations, so no one knows what you're thinking? Do you gossip?
- Sarcasm. Do you make comments that hurt other people's hearts?

We can develop our own character in ways that treat others with dignity and respect, being kind to others and being true to our own values. But even then, we will not please everyone. Not everyone will like us.

The old tale of
The Man, the Boy, and the Donkey
By Aesop

A man and his son were once going with their donkey to market to sell the Donkey. As they were walking along by side by side a countryman passed them and said, "Silly people, what is a donkey for but to ride upon?" So the man put the boy on the donkey, and they went on their way.

But soon they passed a group of men, one of whom said, "See that lazy youngster, he lets his father walk while he rides."

So the man ordered his boy to get off and got on himself. But they hadn't gone far when they passed two women, one of whom said to the other, "Shame on that lazy man to let his poor little son trudge along."

Well, the man didn't know what to do, but at last, he took his boy up before him on the donkey. By this time they had come to the town, and the passersby began to jeer and point at them. The man stopped and asked what they were scoffing at.

The men said, "Aren't you ashamed of yourself for overloading that poor donkey of yours—you and your son? Instead of him carrying both of you, you should be carrying him."

The man and boy got off and tried to think about what to do. They thought and they thought, until at last they cut down a pole, tied the donkey's feet to it, and raised the pole and the donkey to their shoulders. They went along amid the laughter of all who met them until they came to a bridge, when the donkey, getting one of his feet loose, kicked out and caused the boy to drop his end of the pole. In the struggle, the donkey *fell over the bridge, and his forefeet being tied together, he was drowned.*

> *Try to please everyone,*
> *and you will please no one.*

What would you have to give up for everyone to like you?

In the Aesop tale, we see that trying to please everyone is impossible. Think about the people in your life that do not seem to like you. What would you have to change about yourself to become someone they would like? Is that even possible? If you did change all of that, would you even recognize yourself? Would you like yourself at that point? Sometimes we have to release the idea that we will be liked by that person and stop trying. However, I do not mean we stop being kind and civil. What I mean is you stop blaming yourself for trying to be something you will never be. Instead, be kind, be polite, even be friendly, and loving, but stop begging them to like you. That is on them, not on you. Be likable as far as it depends on you and let the rest go.

Love must be sincere. Hate what is evil; cling to what is good. Be devoted to one another in love. Honor one another above yourselves. Never be lacking in zeal, but keep your spiritual fervor, serving the Lord. Be joyful in hope, patient in affliction, faithful in prayer. Share with the Lord's people who are in need. Practice hospitality.

Bless those who persecute you; bless and do not curse. Rejoice with those who rejoice; mourn with those who mourn. Live in harmony with one another. Do not be proud, but be willing to associate with people of low position. Do not be conceited.

Do not repay anyone evil for evil. Be careful to do what is right in the eyes of everyone. If it is possible, as far as it depends on you, live at peace with everyone. Do not take revenge, my dear friends, but leave room for God's wrath, for it is written: "It is mine to avenge; I will repay,"[l] says the Lord. On the contrary:

"If your enemy is hungry, feed him;
if he is thirsty, give him something to drink. In doing this, you will heap burning coals on his head."
Do not be overcome by evil,
but overcome evil with good.
Romans 12:9-21

In Summary

You have the right to not be liked by everyone. No one is universally liked by everyone. You can check to see if you have put barriers to likability that may make others not want to be around you. But if we are kind and respectful to others and still they do not like us, it is okay. We have the right to stay true to who we are and not try to change to please everyone else. We do not have to be liked by everyone. As far as it depends on you, live at peace with everyone, overcome evil with good.

In conclusion, the purpose of this book

At the beginning of this book, I said, "Life is hard." Throughout these pages, you have seen how the lingering effects of past bullying, abuse, trauma, trouble, or chaos can negatively affect today's ability to make good decisions, today's relationships, and today's ability to have joy. You have been shown your basic rights as a human and what that means in a healthy life. If you address the fundamental emotional, physical, and intellectual principles presented in this book, you can have a healthier life. By living the principles of a healthy lifestyle, you can live your very best life, unhindered by the debilitating effects of past traumas.

If you apply these principles of respecting your own rights and the rights of others, it can literally change the course of your life and have a positive effect on people around you. If you apply all the ideas in this book you will discover a revolution inside, a return to something even more powerful than happiness. That is the presence of peace.

By taking a positive and proactive approach toward learning the skills of keeping calm, you can open up opportunities to bring changes for the better for yourself and others; to improve confidence, and resilience. It may take some effort and time, but by making the decision to live calmly you can truly make changes that YOU want, that will take you to places you have always wanted to go, mentally, physically and spiritually.

In closing, I want to remind you that I have posted many free resources for you to continue your journey toward growth and healing on my website at FaithfulHabits.com/Fundamentals Please access these free resources.

Afterword

_____

Faith's Story

The rights I never knew I had.

Human rights were not something I knew existed. Decades of my life were spent living with trauma. I grew up in a Christian and abusive home. Christian and abusive are two words that should not be together, but they were a part of my childhood experience. I grew up in the midst of extreme poverty, occasional homelessness, and all kinds of abuse. In fact, growing up as an abused child, I had it beaten into me that I had no rights. As the youngest, everyone else in my family had more power than me. Those who were bigger and more powerful could do what they wanted to me and there was no protection for me and no way for me to escape their abuse. Healthy patterns of living are important to me now because I grew up in a home with dysfunction, bullying, abuse, trauma, and chaos. I learned from a young age that we were never to talk about our family life to anyone. That was beaten into me so strongly, I would not have even told you what we had for lunch. We spent those years never letting anyone get to know us; we lived isolated. Abuse thrives in isolation.

Hard life lessons in those early years taught me the importance of kindness because I knew what it felt like to be treated unkindly. I valued gentleness because I had been treated with violence. I was wary of 'love' because it was just a word the abusers used as they were hurting me. I found joy when I was alone and in nature. Peace was around me as I enjoyed trees and flowers, wind and sky. I learned the value of calm because in that one skill I could be stronger than those who abused me. My control of my emotions strengthened daily as I figured out how to survive life with trauma. But outward calm is not enough.

What a healthy, functional life was like was unknown to me as a child. I only knew the isolated chaos of my experiences. I did not know I had a right to be safe and protected. I did not know I had a right to my own thoughts, feelings, and opinions. In fact, I felt rebellious for even daring to have my own values and beliefs, even though I rarely risked speaking of them. I was unfamiliar with my rights as a human. As an adult, God took me through a process of healing and growth. It took me a long time to understand that I had rights and that I could exercise those rights.

I didn't know I had rights, but there are four things I have always known, even from my earliest memories. First, I have always known that God is. What could be known about God was plain to me as a child because God has made it plain to us. For since the creation of the world God's invisible qualities— his eternal power and divine nature—have been clearly seen, being understood from what has been made. I could see His handiwork all around me. All the plants and trees and the intricacies of their beauty and diversity tell me of God. So, I have always known that God is.

The second thing I have always known is that God loves me. I could see it in the nature around me, in the way that He has created the world to give us delight. I see that God loves us in the color of flowers. Whether purple or yellow or pink or white, such a huge array of colors. What is the purpose of color but to bring delight to our hearts? We are created to respond to beauty, take pleasure in beauty. Watching trees, the sight of all the different shapes leaves dancing in the wind, has always spoken to me of God's love for me. Food could just be for nourishment—and it is—but food is also for delight. Our nourishment comes in such a wide variety of colors and flavors and smells and textures. Later, I read the Bible, which is filled with messages of His love.

The third thing I have always known is that I am safe in His care. In the midst of the chaos around me as a little girl—dealing with abuse, poverty, and

155

constantly moving—I knew I was safe in God's care. No matter what happened, He was there with me, loves me, and cares for me. My present and my eternity was/is safe with Him.

The fourth thing that I have always known is that although God is, God loves me, and I am safe in his care, these truths do not keep me from getting hurt. I was hurt in body and heart a lot as a little girl. I was abused by the very people who should have protected me. Sometimes they behaved in ways that were loving and nurturing, but I did not rely on that. I knew the betrayal of abuse would always be a part of my experience with them. My family all worked as migrant farm laborers in fields and orchards. I started working full-time at age of three. We often experienced discrimination and rejection from people around us. Also, I experienced ridicule and rejection from other kids in schools as the new kid, the poor kid who did not know what other kids knew and did not have what other kids had. I experienced the glaring disapproval of adults in grocery stores when we shopped after a hard day's work, still in our dirty work clothes, to buy tonight's supper with today's wages.

My understanding of how the world works is that God cherishes being loved and He gave us free will so that we could choose to love Him or choose not to. That ability to choose or choose not to is a precious thing. When we freely choose to love God, it is glorious. But God will not make us love Him; He invites us to love Him. He gave us free will. We get to choose how we will live and what we will value. People therefore sometimes use their free will to hurt themselves and hurt others. I was hurt a lot as a child by the choices of others. When I say that I am safe in God's care, I know that eternally I am safe. When I die, I will go to be with Him in heaven, in that glorious presence. Everything my heart desires is there: my heart desires Him.

Where was God when I was wrongly hurt as a child? God was nurturing me, giving me the strength to endure the hurt. He was there holding my heart. Why did He not stop a little girl from being abused? He is all-powerful; He could have prevented my pain. He chose not to stop it, but He gave me something better, the ability to endure, the resilience to live through it. Then, later in life, He gave me a healing process that healed all of those wounds from my childhood. More than that, He gave me the heart to help others who are in pain. A major part of my adult life is devoted to helping others who are in pain.

I am a mental health counselor theorist in that I have studied in graduate school the theories of dysfunction and of healing and know the ways we can be psychologically healed. I know God designed us so that we can heal. I am a person who has experienced suffering and healed through it. So, when I have a client in front of me who talks about the depth of their wounds and the trauma they have endured, it resonates with me. I know what suffering feels like, but more importantly, I know what it feels like to heal and therefore I can hold hope for them. I can tell them I used to have Post-Traumatic Stress Disorder, PTSD, but I do not have it anymore. I dealt with PTSD intensely for decades, but it has been gone now for decades too.

My experience shows me that when life is in chaos, God is here with me in the midst of that chaos, comforting my heart. Being safe in God's care does not mean He is going to protect me from the things that are going on in the world. It means He protects my heart and my mind. He gives me a way out, gives me a way to be resilient.

A lot of my life has been uncertain and difficult. But I have seen God's love and care in the hard places. When I would call out to him, He would comfort my heart and calm my mind. I read His Word and the words of comfort for other people who have struggled contained within. When I am connected to God's people in church groups and home Bible study groups, these people care about me. We are made to be connected to others in the body of Christ. It is God's love with flesh on.

God loves me even when life is not what I like. God seems to be more concerned with my character development than with my comfort. I tend to be more concerned with my comfort. I like to be comfortable, but it is during uncomfortable times that my character can develop. In those times, I get to choose if am I going to stay true to God, true to my integrity. Am I going to do what is right and proper even when things are hard? I get to choose whether I am going to love and trust God when life is hard.

Jesus is the way. In John 3:16 it stated that "God so loved the world that he sent his only son that whosoever believes in him should not perish but have eternal life." I find that such a wonderfully comforting statement. The "whosoever" means this offer is open to me. It's open to anybody and everybody. No one is too bad or too wrong or too different. God made all of us. The offer is something we have to accept in order to have the eternal life He offers. When we accept Jesus as Savior and Lord, we are agreeing with God that we have done wrong. Confessing to him what we have done and accepting him into our lives as Lord and Savior gives us salvation. The Lord part means that then I want to obey Him. He is not going to make me obey Him, but because I love Him and because He loves me, I want to obey. So, I spend time reading His Word. I spend time with His people, so I am connected and growing more like Him.

This invitation to abundant life is open to anyone and everyone. Not everyone chooses to accept Jesus as Lord and Savior, but that is who He is in my life. He is my savior, my lord, my friend, and my guide to a healthy life.

The fundamental principles I taught you in this book will help you tremendously to have a healthier life. They will help you to understand your rights and your value as you go through the trials of life. But the really deep calm, that solid, unshakable peace welling from the depth inside of you, that comes from knowing, loving, and following Jesus.

Other books by Faith Winters

Are you ready to make lasting change?

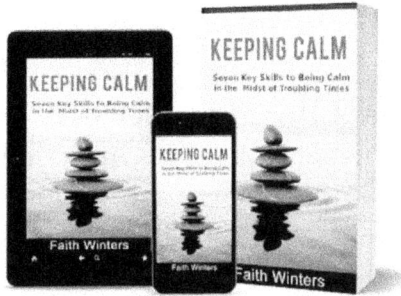

Would you like to face life's troubles with confidence?

These seven skills can transform your life!

When you read this book you will discover how to unlock the secrets of how naturally calm people:

- Have a calmer, happier life
- Make better decisions
- Get rid of constant anxiety
- Lower the effects of stress
- Get better rest and sleep

If you apply all the skill in this book you can be a calm person more powerfully in control of yourself and able to move through life with confidence, no matter what is going on around you.

Trauma Healing Series Outline

www.TraumaHealingSeries.com

This **Trauma Healing Series** explores the differences between a healthy, functional life and a wounded life impacted by the lingering effects of bullying, abuse, trauma, neglect, domestic violence, substance use, and chaos. The series is designed to help lower the barriers that hinder growth and healing so you can move forward toward the freedom of thriving.

> *Trauma is any disturbing experience* that results in significant fear, helplessness, dissociation, confusion, or other disruptive feelings intense enough to have a long-lasting negative effect on a person's attitudes, behavior, and other aspects of functioning. Traumatic events may challenge a person's view of the world as a reasonable, safe, and predictable place.

Many individuals experience trauma during their lifetimes. Although some people exposed to trauma demonstrate few lingering symptoms, other people—especially those who have experienced repeated, chronic, or multiple traumas—are more likely to have many struggles and after-effects, including emotional distress, substance abuse, and physical and mental health problems.

Many individuals who seek help and recovery have histories of trauma. But they often do not recognize the impact their trauma has had on their lives. Either they do not draw connections between their past trauma and their current struggles, or they may try to avoid thinking about hard times altogether. Time alone does not heal most trauma; healthy processing is a part of the healing dynamic.

> ***Processing the past*** *is the act of making sense of an experience and putting it to rest, which includes achieving the resolution needed to move on from a traumatic experience. If some aspect of trauma is not processed, it may continue to cause problems in the present until it can be put to rest.*

Books in the Trauma Healing Series

Trauma Healing Series - Book 1

FUNDAMENTALS

Escape the Lingering Effects
of Bullying, Abuse or Trauma

By learning your fundamental human rights, developing inner awareness of your strengths, and understanding the contrast to past chaos you will step into a life with security, significance, and happiness. Explore how to have more peace within yourself, better relationships with others, and more freedom and contentment, no matter what is going on around you.

Trauma Healing Series - Book 2

RESTORATION

Living as Designed, in Joy and Peace

You are designed to have peace and joy and be able to heal from the wounds of life. Look deeply into your uniqueness. Put to rest the old wounds that hinder your healing and trap you into painful patterns of responding to life. By exploring and adopting healthy patterns instead, you will live your best life after trauma. You will have restoration.

Trauma Healing Series - Book 3

CONNECTIONS

Master the Art of Relationship

When you do what it takes to develop wholesome social habits and essential boundary skills, you can have good relationships at home, at work, and with friends, family, and that special someone, no matter what your past relationships were like. By learning key skills for a healthy lifestyle and safe, healthy relationships, you will unlock the power of community to discover your connected place in the world.

Trauma Healing Series - Book 4

ABUNDANCE

Create Confidence, Contentment and Happiness

You can have the freedom of contentment, recognizing and enjoying the abundance of life around you. Contentment is not the fulfillment of what you want but the realization of what you already have. By using the principles of abundance in this book, you will derive riches that go far beyond the temporary rewards of success and create lasting happiness in any situation.